CHAPTER ONE
Introduction

You Can (Help) Save The World

Alex R Oliver

Published by Beecroft Books, 2021.

YOU CAN (HELP) SAVE THE WORLD

First edition. January 13, 2021.

ISBN: 978-1393196549

Written by Alex R Oliver.

I DON'T KNOW ABOUT you, but sometimes when I contemplate climate change, the loss of the rain forest, the burning of Australia, increasing natural disasters, beloved animals now going extinct, and the threat of our Earth becoming uninhabitable for our children or our grandchildren, I feel physically sick with dread and despair.

There never seems to be any good news, does there?

We hope that our governments will get their acts together to save us, but they end up being part of the problem - short sighted, driven by profit and the drive to get re-elected next time.

Manufacturers and corporations involved in pollution and fossil fuels and deforestation *should* realize it can't go on this way, or we will all die. They should be cleaning up their act, switching to alternatives that would help fix this crisis. But instead they double down on being evil and lie about it to us to keep us buying.

Sometimes it seems hopeless, and I know a lot of people who feel so powerless to do anything to change the oncoming extinction of humanity, that they don't want to hear about it any more. They just want to be allowed to enjoy what life they have left before it all gets even worse. They want to be allowed to fiddle while Rome burns, or - like the band on the Titanic - to carry on playing while the ship goes down.

What can we do, after all? Us normal people, who go to work and worry about our bills and our cars and our children, who don't have time or expertise to solve all the problems of the world? Is there really anything we can do to save the world when all the people who have the power are not?

Well, as Nelson Mandela says:

May your choices reflect your hopes, not your fears.

And if you'll excuse a Tolkien nerd her whimsy - because Tolkien taught me everything I know about hope:

Oft hope is born when all is forlorn.

What can we do? I know 'snowflake' has become something of an insult these days, standing for someone who is sensitive and easily upset. But I remember that when you get enough snowflakes in one place, you get an avalanche. And an avalanche is powerful enough to sweep great institutions away. Individually, we may be weak, but together we are very strong.

During the coronavirus crisis, we've had direct evidence of how much it affects the country when the public as a whole changes its behaviour. Everyone is told to stay at home and only make necessary journeys, and the air clears, pollution falls like a stone, and the petro-chemical industry trembles. The economy staggers. The government scrambles to keep up.

This is power, and we can utilize this power, if there are enough of us acting together. You too can (help) save the world, and that's a hope worth clinging on for.

DRAMATIC INTRODUCTION over, I should probably introduce myself.

Who am I and what are my qualifications for writing a book like this?

Well, I'm nobody really. I'm just an ordinary suburban housewife from Cambridgeshire in the UK. I'm married, I have two grown up children called Rose and Reed (we went for a botanical theme,) and I've written a number of books of fiction. Mostly romance novels, but some SF/F and a couple of cozy mysteries. About twenty five of them have been published, but in America, so you probably won't have heard of me even if I did tell you my pen name.

That gives me a certain amount of practice at expressing myself in writing and finishing the task of writing a book.

It doesn't give me a lot of authority when it comes to telling you how to help save the planet.

But like I said, the people with authority are not doing the job, so the rest of us have to muddle through on our own.

I don't want to denigrate the experts here. There are lots of people who are spending their lives researching soil science, climate change, etc. There are people who are giving talks to government bodies in attempts to form the new eco-friendly policies of the future. People are discovering how to turn deserts back into farms and forests. Other people are working on turning your windows into solar panels, or figuring out ways of making green energy more efficient and less dependent on rare metals. There are people campaigning for everything from polarbears to standing against pipelines. Experts are wonderful people, from whom we can learn, and for whom humanity should be more grateful.

However, experts don't need any advice from me to know which sub-committee of parliament they should be addressing. Experts can talk directly to people in government. They can get grants to study stuff more. They can buy land and run experiments and write papers about the results.

We can't do that. The question is, what can we, the non-expert masses do to help?

As I said earlier, I'm a writer, so for me the gateway drug into eco-consciousness was a fiction genre called Solarpunk. I was feeling very low and hopeless, and I was a little angry at fiction because instead of offering me escape and happy endings, it was offering me Game of Thrones.

Looking for something a little less grimdark, I stumbled across solarpunk. If 'punk' is a symbol of rebellion, solarpunk is a rebellion against hopelessness. It's a movement that dares to hope that the future will be better than the past. It puts a finger up at the suggestion that we should go wailing into that long goodnight and suggests that maybe we should plant a garden instead.

Solarpunk envisages a future where society has replaced its dependence on fossil fuels by green, renewable energy. Where cities grow their own food on the rooftops, and their inhabitants cycle to work among gardens. Solarpunk's future is one of repair - we haven't just slowed climate change, we have reversed it. The deserts are being reclaimed. Lost species of animals are regaining their territories. The oceans are clean. And while, perhaps, nobody has their own car any more, and absolutely nobody has a private jet, it's easy to get around on public transport, but it's easier still, and more rewarding to live locally, eat locally and come closer to your own community.

I wanted to learn more about this. But I hadn't spent more than a few weeks in solarpunk areas of the internet before I heard about the things that many solarpunk fans were doing to bring this green utopia about in real life. I heard about how terribly plastic was messing up our world, and the movement to go zero waste, and I heard about permaculture, with its emphasis on earth care, people care and fair share.

A little light came on in the bleakness of my heart. I was learning that our future was not hopeless after all. Life could continue, and more than continue, there was a way in which it might improve.

As often happens, when you start to have an interest in things, you start noticing that thing all over the place. The first really significant step on my journey came when I was shopping in the Oxfam charity shop, where I buy my coffee. They had a display of recycled products, in the middle of which was a small, attractive blue book with a picture of a whale on the front. Called How to Give Up Plastic: A Guide to Changing the World, One Plastic Bottle at a Time[1], by Will McCallum, the Head of Oceans at Greenpeace, the book might as well have been decorated with a personally calligraphed label shouting READ ME. I took it home and did just that.

With the guidance of this book, I went through each room in my house and figured out how to eliminate or at least reduce the use of plastic or plastic-wrapped products in each one.

The book was simple, but the process of putting it into practice was more complicated. It took me the better part of six months. Many of the instructions lead me down yet more avenues of testing and decision making, exploring, discovering resources and tutorials on the internet and experimenting with my own solutions, before I was satisfied. Over the section called 'Life Without Plastic,' I'm going to share with you what I learned in the process, in a way that will hopefully make it easy for you to do a similar thing, but with less effort.

The process of de-plasticking my life was intensive and absorbing. I enjoyed the challenge and the constant learning about new ways of doing things. Once I had gone through every room in my house and found non-plastic alternatives for the things that I used to buy, though, I was feeling so accomplished and so very much like I was actually making a difference, that I didn't want to say, "Right, I've finished now."

I found myself looking out for the next thing I could do better. I had tackled the use of fossil fuels to create plastic, and the role plastic plays in cluttering up the world, clogging the earth and sea. But there was a lot more to do. Climate change is not just due to plastic use. There was over-consumption of greenhouse-gas emitting fuels to heat the house, to drive the car. Was there anything I could do about this? In the 'Living More Sustainably' section I'll let you know what I found out about this.

And of course, once I was down that rabbit hole I kept finding out *more* ways in which we are currently killing the planet. Agriculture!

---

1.   https://www.amazon.co.uk/How-Give-Plastic-spokesperson-anti-plastic/dp/0241363217

Did you know that food growing contributes at least 14% to the world's emissions of greenhouse gasses, and some sources make that closer to 50%? I hadn't known that! I'd always looked at farm land as part of the solution—beautiful, well-tended and all around praiseworthy. Nope. Turns out that in addition to contributing to global warming, agriculture as it now exists is killing the planet's soil and contributing to desertification.

It was lucky that I only discovered this *from* the people who already had a solution for it, or it would have given me further sleepless nights. But no, this was where Permaculture and its' big brother Restorative Agriculture came back into the picture in a big way.

In the 'Solutions in the Soil' section I'll dive into permaculture - what it is, why it's important and how you can learn to use it to create zero-waste solutions to almost anything. You may come out of it feeling that you want to take up gardening in a sustainable way, or enthused to make your own community more food-secure and self-sufficient.

My back-garden food forest is currently planted and growing. I'd be the first to admit that I don't yet really know what I'm doing with it, although I've had several meals out of it by now. I can, however point you at the people from whom I learned what I know, so that you can listen to people who do know what they're talking about.

In the last section, 'Broadening Our Reach,' I'll give some examples of places you can go on to once you too have sorted out your lifestyle, learned to garden and are looking for the next big challenge. Changing the world can only really be done when there are lots of people all doing what we can. So, even if you are - like me - the world's greatest introvert, eventually you'll reach a point where you can only go forward by becoming involved in the rest of society. Fortunately these don't have to be too scary, and they can start on the internet. Fellow introverts, we can creep out of our shells by careful and safe degrees. Extroverts, this is your time to shine! Get out there, make friends, make connections and societies. Change the world!

One of the things I've learned over the course of this now two year journey, is that permaculture has three principles; Earth Care, People Care and Fair Share. It's part of the permaculture ethos to share what you've learned and what you've gained while you were growing, so that others can also learn and gain, and we can all become full of abundance together. I offer you this book in that spirit, in the hope that you too will be comforted and inspired by the thought that it's not too late for you, yes, you individually, to (help to) save the world.

CHAPTER TWO
Life without plastic

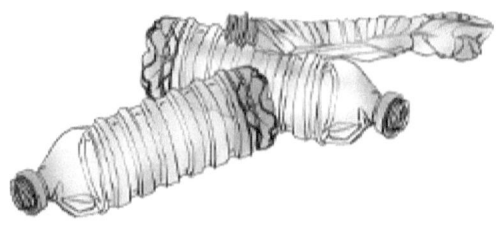

"WE HAVE TO ACT. WE have to act now to try and clear up some of the appalling damage we have made to the ocean ... and that is going to require positive action"
Sir David Attenborough

According to PlasticOceans.uk from which I took the above quote by Sir David Attenborough, 8 million tonnes of plastic enter the oceans every year, half of which - 4 million tonnes - consists of single-use plastic. That is, water bottles that you bought and threw away. Those flimsy plastic bags you put your vegetables in in the supermarket and then throw away at home. The tear off film on cartons of salad or take-away sandwiches, the wrappers of biscuits, and crisp packets, and the bags that multi-pack bags of whatever come in. And many, many other products that we don't even notice until we train ourselves to.

This plastic accumulates in great islands of trash that chokes sea-birds and dolphins, gets into the stomachs of fish and turtles, breaks up into smaller particles which end up in the guts of the food that we eat. As if that wasn't enough, it acts as a sponge for other chemicals that are toxic to human life. We eat these when we eat the plastic-filled fish or seafood brought out of the ocean's increasingly dirty water.

'Microplastics' are plastic that has been torn or shredded or disintegrated into such small pieces that we can't see them with the human eye. A prime example of these is the microbeads that are in so much make-up, and exfoliating creams and face-washes. They're so small you can barely feel them, but even at that size they're a problem. They wash straight out to sea, where they harbour bad chemicals. They get eaten by creatures—including ourselves—who can't digest them. They get into the beaches, and into the soil, where they will stay for thousands of years, because nothing that lives on the planet knows how to turn them back into anything useful.

And even though plastic pollution in the ocean is an ongoing environmental disaster, it's not the only problem. We can't consider ourselves safe here on the land either. Plastic bottles and bags litter our streets, get into drainage ditches,causing floods. Plastic-fibered wipes get into our sewage system, forming impassable blockages that have to be hacked apart by hand by intrepid sewage workers. Plastic waste forms half our landfill area by volume, never rotting down, never going away, just accumulating tonne by tonne until we'll end up with no land left to live on.

Instead of leaving it to lie around cluttering up the place, we could incinerate it, maybe? Well... we could. But that just results in extra greenhouse gasses released during the burning process.

And that's just the waste end of the problem of plastic. We focus a lot on plastic in the ocean or in the landfill, because that's where we can point to pictures of dead animals and the most hardened of hearts will have to agree that this is terrible, but plastic is also a major polluter of the earth *when it's being made.*

Before you've even bought it, plastic has contributed to climate change, simply because it is made from fossil fuel.

"Plastic production is already responsible for 5% of greenhouse gas emissions – gases that are warming the planet and causing more extreme weather.

These gases are released during oil and gas drilling, and as a result of energy consumption in the plastics processing industry."

...

"Unabated, plastic will soon be a **bigger contributor to climate change than aviation and shipping** put together."

— Friends of the Earth

(Let's pass quickly over the fact that plastic, by virtue of being made of fossil fuel is inextricably linked with all the dodgy stuff first world countries have been up to in pursuit of oil—the wars and the coups and so forth.)

I'm not going to go into giving you facts and figures about all this stuff here, because it's easy enough to read up on it on the internet, and I encourage you to do so. I think it's a good idea for you to fact check this stuff yourself, because the process of becoming a more ecologically aware person involves a lot of learning, and I'm going to assume that's something that you enjoy.

I will, however fling some reputable sources your way. Check out what Friends of the Earth[1] have to say, or take a quick tour of the articles that Greenpeace have amassed about Plastic Pollution[2]. All 120 of them!

If you're anything like me, you're already impatient because this is old news to you—you wouldn't have picked up a book on how to help save the world if you weren't aware that plastic was a problem. You're

---

1.   https://friendsoftheearth.uk/plastics

2.   https://www.greenpeace.org.uk/?s=plastic+pollution

probably already one of the 17% of people who put the effort in to properly recycle your plastic waste in the UK.

If that's the case, well done. You are clearly already doing more than most people, and you can rightfully be pleased with yourself. But brace yourself, because the truth is that the UK 'recycles' most of its plastic waste by just sending it abroad[3]. Before 2018 we used to send it to China, but China eventually put their foot down and refused to take any more. Now we send it to Malaysia and Turkey. Or we incinerate it. Recycling is honestly not the catch all solution we were led to believe

I had to take a little break to be disgusted by that when I first found out. "Well, what the heck am I supposed to do then?" I exclaimed to the empty kitchen. "This is hopeless. It's absolutely hopeless!"

Soon, however, I was back on the internet looking for a solution. The solution that presented itself was pretty radical, but I could not deny that it would work:

To prevent contributing to plastic pollution in future, I have to stop buying new plastic things.

If I stopped buying things that involved plastic - things that were made of plastic, or wrapped in plastic - not only would I immediately stop adding to the world's plastic waste problem through my own waste, but I would send a message to the manufacturers of plastic things and plastic packaging that there was no longer profit to be made in these things.

Again, I am assuming that although I as a single individual will not make a big difference, if we all do these things as separate individuals, that will end up being a massive group effort. Companies will notice it.

Companies are, in fact, already noticing that consumers want eco-friendly items, *and* many companies are becoming aware that fossil fuels are running out and that if they wish to continue trading, they're going to need to change. We've never had a better time than now to put the pressure on them, via our buying habits and our feedback.

---

3.   https://www.bbc.co.uk/news/science-environment-49827945

If we just attend rallies and write letters to companies to say 'Plastic is bad!' but we continue to buy it, they're likely to ignore it. If we stop buying it in droves, they'll take notice and adapt. The customer may not be always right, but sometimes it's worth flexing our buying power anyway.

Now obviously, it's easy to say "I must stop buying new plastic things." But given how ubiquitous they are in our society, it's much harder to do. I'm not giving up my medicine, which comes in a plastic applicator, or blister-packed painkillers. My computer keyboard and screen are plastic. As is my debit card. As is cash money these days. All of those are things that I can't do without, and they're only a small sample of essential plastic items. As the world stands, it's impossible to get rid of all plastic from your life immediately.

So I'm going to rephrase my realization in a more manageable and less holier-than-thou way:

To reduce my contribution to plastic pollution in future, and encourage companies to produce less of it, I have to use as little plastic as possible, *especially single use plastic.*

I'm singling out single use plastic here, because a plastic bag you use to bring home three potatoes from the supermarket and then throw away is a lot more of a waste of the earth's finite resources and a lot more of a contributor to pollution than is—for example—a plastic bucket you use every day for 50 years and then give to your child who uses it for another half century.

When it comes to plastic there is a hierarchy of evil, and it's up to us to attack the most wasteful and the least necessary first. We can work up to the hard stuff, and tackle the apparently impossible after that.

So, with the introduction behind us, let's take a look at what we can do to eliminate as much plastic use as we can, without depriving ourselves of anything vital in the process.

Here, I want again to recommend How to Give Up Plastic: A Guide to Changing the World, One Plastic Bottle at a Time, by Will

McCallum[4]. This is the book that started me on my journey. You may find it inspiring too.

In the following sections, we're going to go through the house room by room, and I'll give you a quick run down of what I did to remove the use of plastic from each one.

A quick note, though. If you have plastic items in your house which you use regularly and which are not disposable, don't feel you should throw them out in an attempt to make your house *look* like it's eco-friendly. Throwing out your plastic soap dish and buying a new bamboo one for the aesthetic is kind of wasteful after all.

On the other hand, if you desperately *want* to throw out your current plastic stuff, and that's the step holding you back from committing to being plastic free in future, I wouldn't honestly feel too bad if you did make a little bit of extra waste in the re-jigging process. This is hopefully the first step to a life free of plastic waste entirely. So do what you can, and don't beat yourself up. This process *should* be exciting. A whole new life, and a better one, is waiting for you to start.

---

4.   https://www.barnesandnoble.com/w/how-to-give-up-plastic-will-mccallum/1129853063

The Coat-Rack, aka shopping

THERE ARE SO MANY THINGS the eco-friendly person needs to take with them on a shopping trip that these things have to live somewhere. I suggest assembling your 'I will need this on my shopping trip' items into a kit that lives as close to the door you regularly go in and out of as possible. Hang it with your coat so that you can pick it up as you pass, on the way out of the door.

I'm sure you've heard everything I have to say about shopping already from many different sources, but I'm including it here so that we can deal with the easiest stuff first.

When you go shopping, you do not want to be forced to buy a plastic carrier bag to bring your purchases home in. No matter how much you tell yourself you'll use the carrier bag again, no matter how diligently you store the plastic bag in a plastic bag of plastic bags for later use, you probably won't ever use it again. You've probably already got a hundred plastic bags just like it scrunched up and lurking in a cupboard, so let's make an effort to stop adding more.

You're going to need a reusable bag, and you're going to need to remember to take that reusable bag with you.

Plus—I don't know about you—but if I'm on the way to the supermarket, I often buy so much stuff that I need two or even three bags to bring it home in. It's no good having one reusable bag and then having to buy carriers to fit the rest.

You're going to need at least *three* reusable bags.

I like to use the bags made out of recycled saris which you can buy in Oxfam. They come with their own pocket so you can fold them small, they are a way of recycling waste all on their own, they support charity and they don't weigh very much.

After a long day's shopping, do you like to stop in the coffee shop for a slice of cake and a hot drink? I know I do. Rather than use a plastic coffee cup with a plastic lid which will just be thrown away, take your own reusable cup, save yourself 25p and prevent more plastic from entering the environment. The more of us who do this, the less lids will end up in the gutter.

I'm not here to sell any specific type of reusable cup, so I give you permission to treat yourself by buying whichever one you fancy. I would say, however, that—again—you might want to give consideration to how much it weighs. You're already carrying three bags and a cup and we're not done yet.

Maybe you prefer a cold drink, which has to be drunk with a straw. One of those thick, ice-creamy ones? Buy yourself one of those insulated cups with a straw[5] and see if they'll make it in that for you.

Are you going to be out over lunch-time? How likely is it that you're going to buy a salad or some noodles from a shop on the high street to eat as you go? That food's probably going to come with plastic cutlery, and you don't want your spoon today to end up in the gullet of a sea-bird tomorrow. Maybe you should take a knife, fork and spoon with you so you can refuse the plastic ones when they're offered.

Maybe you're going food shopping?

---

5.   https://www.ebay.co.uk/sch/
    i.html?_from=R40&_trksid=p2047675.m570.l1311.R1.TR10.TRC0.A0.H0.Xinsulated+cup
    +with+.TRS0&_nkw=insulated+cup+with+straw&_sacat=0

Cheese and meat are almost always wrapped in plastic, so instead consider shopping from the deli counter, where you can ask the assistant to give you these items in containers you have brought with you for the purpose. But that means, of course, that you're going to have to take containers with you in your shopping kit. I usually take a couple of light plastic boxes of the sort that are given out by takeaway food shops. These do very well to buy meat, sausages, bacon and cheese.

Now if we look on the rest of the supermarket shelves, we find that onions and oranges come in single-use plastic nets that end up strangling sea creatures. We don't want those. Mushrooms come in plastic punnets. But these things also come loose, with no packaging at all. It would be convenient to have bags to put them in, so we can weigh them and handle them without dropping them all over the place.

I'm afraid we're going to have to carry our own bags here too. In this case, if you've saved all the filmy plastic bags you used to get from the supermarket, you can take a handful of these with you to re-use them. Alternatively you could make or buy yourself some fabric drawstring bags like these.[6]

When I was first experimenting with all this, I saw a roll of what Waitrose claimed were 'compostable' plastic-like filmy bags made of some sort of starch, which I thought would fit inside one of my takeaway containers and be less bulky than the fabric bags. But experimentation proved that they were not compostable in my compost pile. Instead they just sat there looking gross and tangling up the tines of my garden fork, making me have to reach in to the half-decomposed goop and slide them off like particularly disgusting cold used sanitary towels. No thank you. I didn't use them again. Your experience may be different, but I don't recommend them.

---

6.   https://www.ebay.co.uk/itm/
10PCS-Reusable-Mesh-Produce-Bags-Grocery-Fruit-Vegetable-Storage-Shopping-Eco-UK/
183811993166?hash=item2acc0c6e4e:g:rssAAOSw9SdeGC31

And, how could I forget? All this shopping is thirsty work, and the last thing we want is to have to buy bottled water. Not only is that massively contributing to plastic waste, but also to companies thinking that water is something you need to pay for and not a human right. Really, buy yourself an awesome water bottle and take your own water with you out of the tap.

To recap. On your eco-friendly shopping trip, you're taking with you:

- (At least) Three reusable bags
- Reusable coffee cup and/or reusable cold drink cup
- Reusable cutlery or chopsticks
- Takeaway containers for meat and cheese
- Fabric bags for loose fruit and veg
- Full water bottle

That's a lot of stuff! How on earth are you supposed to remember to take all of those things with you every time, when you've been trying to remember to take a water bottle for years and you forget nine times out of ten?

There is a solution, and it's a nice one which will probably make you as happy as it did me. That solution is, buy yourself a basket. (Or a back-pack. Or a large bag of a design of your choice.)

Put all the things in your basket, and leave the basket hanging as close to the front door as possible, where you will inevitably see it as you're going out. If the kit is all prepared and you have to pass it as you go out of the door, and you only have to pick up one item—the basket itself—you're a lot more likely to do it.

When you *return* from your shopping trip, a little more organization is required. You must wash the cups, cutlery and bottle and return them to the basket. You must empty out the bags, fold and put them back into the basket. You must replace the containers with new ones so that the kit is ready to go again. But this is all part of the whole unpacking process you have to go through with any shopping, and quickly becomes a habit.

There's something very satisfying about being able to turn down all that plastic crap we're continually offered at the shops. Your waste bin becomes emptier. Your plastic bag bag stops filling up. Your shopping kit becomes an old friend that you pick up on the way out of the house out of long habit and you really don't miss a thing.

Laundry

THINGS TO SAY ABOUT the Washing of Clothes

We're still in the 'getting rid of plastic' part of the book, rather than the 'living more sustainably' part, so I'm not going to say much about the energy usage of big appliances like the washing machine and the tumble dryer. Right now, we're still looking for disposable plastic items that we want to stop buying.

In the laundry this usually means a bottle of fabric softener and a bottle of laundry washing liquid.

Fabric softener

This one's easy to get rid of. Fabric softener is not actually necessary at all. I was fortunate enough to be alive before fabric softener was invented. So when it first came in I was already predisposed to think, "Well, I don't need that!" And I never have. My clothes are still plenty soft enough, and I'm not suffering from the lack.

Quite apart from never having to throw a plastic softener bottle away ever again, just imagine how many hundreds of pounds you can save if you just stop buying fabric softener from this moment on. One less chemical full of potentially dubious ingredients for you to share your life with.

Laundry liquid.

I considered a number of options when it came to never buying another plastic bottle of laundry detergent.

Conkers

Woman shares how you can make laundry detergent with conkers[7]

As the article says, horse chestnuts (aka conkers) contain a high level of saponins (soap-like chemicals.)

I decided I would try this for myself and report on the results. So I gathered a bag full of conkers last autumn and experimented with using these for laundry. I didn't bother with all the drying and chopping, because I'm all about doing things the easy way. This was my method:

Take 6 large conkers and chop each one into quarters.

Steep for half an hour in 300mls boiling water.

Strain the conkers out of the liquid, and use the liquid as a laundry detergent.

You can steep the same conkers again with more hot water, and that will give you a half strength liquid.

Put any left over liquid in a jam jar in the fridge. It will keep for up to a week.

Put the used up conkers in your green bin or garden compost.

I was personally quite delighted by the fact that foam happened, even in my area of particularly hard water.

However, the resulting clean was not great. The conker-liquid drew dirt out of the fabric but then left it in the water, so when the fabric came out of the machine, it came with balls of grime attached. I had to soak and scrub everything again by hand to get it visibly clean.

The plus side of this was that it removed some dried-on stains that conventional laundry liquid had never touched. The negative side was that it took twice as much water and three times the time to do the

---

7.　　　https://metro.co.uk/2019/10/01/

woman-shares-can-make-laundry-detergent-conkers-10829102/

laundry. I was not impressed enough to do it again, even if conker laundry liquid is free.

If that hasn't put you off, and you want to have a go yourself, I would give the linked article a thorough read. Remember that horse chestnut trees are on the decline and it's important to plant a few of your harvested conkers and nurture them into trees for the generations that come after us.

In theory there is no reason why this liquid can't also be used as hand soap and washing up liquid. I have tried it and been unimpressed—the washing up water goes a murky green colour, and there is no foam. It smells musty. I couldn't get over the feeling that nothing was really clean. I'm going to keep that option in reserve, on the grounds that it might be useful to know about if civilization falls, but right now I would prefer something else.

Soap nuts[8].

Soap nuts are the coating of a seed that grows on the *Sapindus Mukorossi* tree, which grows on the slopes of the Himalayas. This is the traditional detergent of the Indian subcontinent, and is natural, biodegradable, does not harm the environment once it's flushed away out of your washing machine and presumably must be effective if so many people use it.

I haven't tried these myself, so I can't vouch for them one way or another. You can buy them from many places on the internet[9], and they come in a cotton bag rather than a plastic bottle.

My own lack of interest in trying them out has been mainly due to the worry that—as has happened with Quinoa—if Westerners come in with their massive buying power and start buying up the traditional

---

8.   https://www.thenaturalgardener.co.uk/soap_nuts.php

9.   https://www.ethicalsuperstore.com/products/ecozone/
      ecozone-soap-nuts---1kg/?PCode=DSGPESS15&utm_source=bing&utm_medium=cpc&utm
      _campaign=Bing%20shopping%20(Bing)&utm_term=4580977764652512&utm_content=A
      d%20group%20231

resources of less-affluent countries, we may end up driving the prices up to a point where the native people can't afford them any more. That's hardly fair!

I also feel that any gain in eco-friendliness caused by not getting your detergent in a plastic bottle is lost by the fact that it has to be transported half way across the world, with the expenditure of a great deal of tanker or airplane fuel.

If the choice was between foaming nuts that grow on trees, I would give conkers another chance, rather than going for something with such a large transport footprint. Your mileage may differ, however.

Fortunately, foamy nuts are not our only option. There are companies making eco-friendly, biodegradable laundry liquid that either come in glass bottles, or for which you can buy refills so you only ever need to buy a single plastic bottle.

I think it helps if we throw our consumer power behind companies who are trying to do good things. Buying eco, non-plastic products instead of harmful ones is our best way to indicate that the market is looking for eco-friendly options and is willing to spend money on them. So I don't feel bad about buying laundry liquid instead of collecting my own. Not everyone will have access to a conker tree, after all.

I'm fortunate enough to have a hardware shop in my local town which has an Ecover refill station. So laundry liquid is something I can buy from there. I just kept my bottle rather than throwing it out, and when it's empty I take it into town and get it refilled.

Find Your Local Refill Station[10]

If you have no local refill station, you might consider clubbing together with friends and neighbors to buy a bulk container which you can all share, instead. Or buy out of your own pocket, add a little markup for your trouble and become your village's refill store yourself.

Bulk containers from Ecover[11]

---

10.   https://www.ecover.com/store-locator/

I'm sure, like me, you've heard rumors that Ecover tests their products on animals. But on investigation, I found out that the animals in question were tiny water fleas. For my part, I'm not sure how Ecover can know whether or not their cleaning products are safe for release into the water system *without* testing to see if they damage small water microorganisms, so for me this is not the ethical hill I'm prepared to die on.

If you feel more strongly about that, I can also recommend Fill[12].

According to their own website, "Fill is a range of refillable eco laundry & household cleaning products that look cool, work great & reduce packaging waste. Supplied in 500ml screen-printed glass bottles & jars, 10l bag-in-box, 20l post consumer recycled (pcr) refills and returnable bulk 200l (we can also do 600l & 1000l) containers that we pick up and refill for a zero waste closed loop solution."

My main problem with Fill is that they don't always have the item you want in stock. In fact I went on their website today and *none* of their bulk refill big boxes were in stock. That might have been coronavirus related, since I'm writing this in the middle of lockdown. It's worth going to see for yourself whether that's righted itself since the time of publication.

I'm sure that there are other companies out there. Have a look on the Ethical Superstore[13] and see for yourself.

Things to say about the drying of clothes
Tumble-dryer sheets
You know it's bad when it's got a whole subheading of its own.

- Dryer sheets are made of polyester - so you're introducing plastic microfibers into the environment with each use.

---

11.   https://www.ecoverdirect.com/departments/refills.aspx?deptid=RF

12.   https://www.fillrefill.co/

13.   https://www.ethicalsuperstore.com/category/cleaning-and-household/

- Dryer sheets contain potentially harmful chemicals—causing anything from headaches and dizziness to asthma[14].

- Dryer sheets are single-use and only partially biodegradable. They're creating a huge waste problem all on their own.

- And to cap it all off, you don't even need them.

"But Alex," you may be saying to yourself, "I *love* that moment when I get my fresh washing out of the dryer, all soft and scented with perfume. I love basking in the smell and the warmth. It's one of the best moments of my day!"

If that's the case, and that's the point where you say "This much, and no more!" then you *still* don't need tumble-dryer sheets. Instead, you could get yourself some woolen dryer balls. (If I still used my tumble dryer, I would totally get myself a flock of these lovely British wool sheep balls[15] from Little Beau Sheep.) These soften your clothes by gently knocking into them as they tumble. You can drop a few drops of your favorite essential oils onto the balls before putting them into the dryer, where the heat will diffuse the scent through all of your clothes. No plastic microfibers and no toxic chemicals required.

If you're less concerned about smell, and more concerned about softness (particularly if you have given up on fabric softener,) you could substitute a hard plastic dryer ball[16] for the woolen one. These beat

---

14. https://www.ecowatch.com/why-you-need-to-ditch-dryer-sheets-1881714654.html

15.   https://www.littlebeausheep.com/campaign/laundrycare/

16.   https://www.currys.co.uk/gbuk/household-appliances/laundry/laundry-accessories/
    wpro-wba100-tumble-dryer-softening-ball-17316309-pdt.html?istCompanyId=bec25c7e-cbcd-
    460d-81d5-a25372d2e3d7&istFeedId=4d7eb93e-055f-499d-8ee5-1cdcc50d67d1&istItemId=x
    iairpxq&istBid=tztx&srcid=198&cmpid=ppc~gg~2008_PLA_AO_BAU_Hoc3-SDA_Hoc1-
    WHITE+GOODS+ACCESSORIES_MA-WHITE+GOODS+ACCESSORIES_All_G_No

your clothes up even more thoroughly than the woolen ones, resulting in a softer feel. And it's better to buy a couple of plastic balls which you're going to use for decades than it is to buy a plastic bottle of fabric softener and a bunch of plastic-wrapped, plastic dryer sheets every month or so that are just going to go straight to landfill.

OKAY, WE'RE BEGINNING to reach the rooms that require a bit of careful thought and actual changes to our lifestyle now. But the bathroom is one where changing things can be an active pleasure.

If your first reaction was "What have we got in the bathroom that's plastic?" so was mine. But the answer is, "A surprising amount of things."

A short list of stuff in the bathroom that contains plastic, or is contained by a plastic container, goes like this:

Toilet roll, toilet wipes, toilet brush.

Shampoo, conditioner, toothpaste, toothbrushes, liquid soap.

Cosmetics, moisturizer, cosmetic wipes, shaving kit, deodorant.

Menstrual products.

Toilet Roll

So let's start with the toilet roll. Most toilet rolls from the supermarket come in a multipack which is held together by plastic wrap. The plastic wrap is of no use to man nor beast and is destined to be thrown away, where it will go from 'useless' to 'an active menace.' However there are several plastic free alternatives out there.

If you're in a position to buy a large box of 48 rolls at once and store it while you work through it, then your choice is between Who Gives A Crap[17] and Greencane Paper[18]. Both will allow you to set up a

---

17. https://uk.whogivesacrap.org/

18. https://greencane.com/

regular order so that a new box of toilet rolls come to your door every 6-18 weeks depending on your frequency of use. (I was very thankful for my box of Who Gives A Crap paper when the Covid crisis struck and suddenly you couldn't find toilet roll anywhere in the shops.)

Who Gives A Crap wrap their individual rolls in wrapping paper, which makes them easier to store around the house without getting dusty, but which is also a bit of a waste of paper. Greencane do not. Who Gives A Crap donates 50% of their profits toward building toilets and improving sanitation in the developing world. Greencane do not.

There are also choices if you aren't in position to buy a large box and store it. Here the choice is between The Cheeky Panda[19] paper, where you can buy a four pack wrapped in paper, or Ecoleaf[20], which offers a four pack wrapped in compostable film.

I'm just going to get this rant out here, pardon me for a moment, but I effing hate compostable film! It won't compost in my home bin, and you can't be certain that your council will allow it in the green bin either—in which case it'll go to landfill and probably not compost anyway. Sadly compostable film is an idea whose time has not yet come because the infrastructure needed to support it isn't yet in place. But OTOH, you may have a council that does accept it in your green bin, and you may prefer the idea of a roll that's made in the UK—which doesn't come with the shipping guilt attached.

If Ecoleaf was wrapped in paper, that would be the one for me. But as it is, I'm personally happy with Who Gives A Crap. Your mileage may vary.

Toilet Wipes

---

19.   https://www.ethicalsuperstore.com/products/the-cheeky-panda/
the-cheeky-panda-plastic-free-bamboo-toilet-tissue---4-rolls/?PCode=DSGPESS15&utm_sour
ce=bing&utm_medium=cpc&utm_campaign=Bing%20shopping%20(Bing)&utm_term=458
0977765776024&utm_content=Ad%20group%20%231

20.   https://www.ethicalsuperstore.com/products/ecoleaf/

I will admit that I loved my toilet wipes. It was a real wrench having to give them up. But the truth is that even the ones that claim to be flushable actually do not dissolve in water. They just go down the pipes until they find a narrow bit where they congeal with any fat that might be in the water and form huge, disgusting 'fatbergs' that cause the sewage pipes to burst. Here's a lovely little piece about the environmental cost of toilet wipes in the Guardian[21].

Even if they don't create a fatberg in the sewers, and they *do* disintegrate, sadly what they disintegrate into is plastic microfibers—see everything I said in the laundry about the environmental costs of those!

I believe there are wipes which are flushable, biodegradable and contain no plastic, such as Twipes[22]. This is another product you can buy on subscription, and you get two, 100 sheet, packets per month.

The packs come wrapped in recyclable plastic, though, and we're trying to get rid of plastic. Their competitors, Jackson Reece Kinder by Nature[23] Wipes, and The Cheeky Panda baby wipes[24] suffer from the same problem, so to my mind that doesn't really work.

So yeah, I'm sorry, but toilet wipes have to go. On the plus side, we managed for centuries without them, and we can manage without them again. And if paper is too harsh on your most delicate areas, we'll have a chat about 'Family Cloth' in the Personal Hygiene section of the Living More Sustainably chapter.

Toilet Brush

---

21.   https://www.theguardian.com/environment/2016/nov/20/the-eco-guide-to-wet-wipes

22.   https://www.twipes.co.uk/

23.   https://www.standard.co.uk/shopping/esbest/beauty/organic-natural/
        best-ecofriendly-alternatives-to-wet-wipes-a3838076.html

24.   https://www.standard.co.uk/shopping/esbest/beauty/organic-natural/
        best-ecofriendly-alternatives-to-wet-wipes-a3838076.html

If you currently have a plastic toilet brush, and it's fine, that's great. Keep on using it until it wears out. You may well get decades of use out of it, and that's better than just throwing it away.

When it does wear out, you can replace it with an all natural brush made of wood and plant or animal bristles, like this one from Peace With The Wild[25], or this one from Be A Shade Greener[26].

Shampoo and conditioner

Most people buy their shampoo and conditioner from the supermarket where it comes contained in a plastic bottle. And okay, we don't get through these terribly fast, but it all mounts up.

There are several options for replacing these with zero-plastic items:

1. Refill your bottles with liquid shampoo and conditioner from a bulk buy shop.

This is a great option if you happen to have a bulk buy shop which sells shampoo and conditioner near to you. I do, so this is the one I go for now.

A nice thing about this option is that you can get yourself some lovely bottles from the charity shop to decant your shampoo and conditioner into. A bathroom looks extra-special when the bottles on the shelf by the shower are things you chose for their beauty. I personally have my shampoo in an old-fashioned stoneware ginger-beer bottle, and my conditioner in a fancy glass bottle that once held liqueur.

2. Solid shampoo and conditioner

There are a wide variety of solid shampoos and conditioner bars available on the internet[27], and if you happen to have a Lush[28] on your

---

25.   https://www.peacewiththewild.co.uk/product/
       eco-living-natural-bristle-toilet-brush-and-holder/

26.   https://www.beashadegreener.com/eco-friendly-wooden-toilet-brush/

27.   https://www.ebay.co.uk/sch/
       i.html?_nkw=solid+shampoo+and+conditioner&norover=1&mkevt=1&mkrid=710-55005-1

high street, you can also get them there. These are basically solid bars of soap-like products that you can lather under water and rub into your hair. Because they're solid, they can come wrapped in paper or even completely unwrapped. Get yourself a couple of nice dishes from the charity shop to keep these in when they're not being used, and again your bathroom will look more decorative than it did when you had those awful generic plastic bottles all over it.

3. *Make your own shampoo and conditioner*

I have not tried this one, so I can't recommend anything, although I will say that I've seen people whose hair suffered very badly from the baking soda treatment recommended in Good Housekeeping[29]. As a child, my mother used to wash my hair in washing up liquid, so the Castille soap recipe on that link may be fine. I don't know. I'm sure there are many people out there with recipes of their own just waiting to be googled.

I didn't try making my own because I skipped straight to the hardcore option first and went No Poo[30].

4. *The No Poo method.*[31]

'No Poo' just stands for 'no shampoo.'

When you think about it, it's rather odd that we have to shampoo our hair. Animals' coats stay healthy and clean without periodic

---

8975-0&mkcid=2&keyword=solid+shampoo+and+conditioner&crlp=_&MT_ID=&geo_id
=&rlsatarget=kwd-81638852993362%3Aloc-188&adpos=&device=c&mktype=&loc=13313
6&poi=&abcId=&cmpgn=352759313&sitelnk=&adgroupid=1306219999789722&network
=s&matchtype=e&msclkid=fd3ffae1a82418c16de8a412d7d628d4&ul_noapp=true

28.   https://uk.lush.com/search/site/
solid%20shampoo?f%5B0%5D=bundle%3A%28knot_wrap%20OR%20product_display%20
OR%20gift_box%20OR%20spa_treatment%29

29.   https://www.goodhousekeeping.com/beauty/hair/a20705785/
homemade-shampoo-conditioner-recipes/

30.   https://www.nopoomethod.com/

31.   *https://www.nopoomethod.com/*

lathering up. Our ape ancestors probably didn't wash their hair with shampoo and conditioner. So why should we?

Once this question started to be asked, a lot of people started experimenting with not washing their hair at all, and many of them discovered that after a month or so of acclimatizing, their hair became healthier and glossier than ever.

I tried this myself—I simply washed my hair as normal, but I only used warm water. I didn't add any shampoo or conditioner.

After about four days, my hair felt disgustingly greasy, and I felt unwashed and rotten. But I had heard that this was a part of the process. It was just my hair re-establishing its normal and necessary level of protective sebum and that it would sort itself out if given the time to do so.

I bought myself a boar-bristle brush, which was supposed to help spread the sebum up the hair shaft, and brushing with that certainly made it feel better.

Toward the end of a month of acclimatizing, I went on holiday to a soft water area, and when I washed my hair in the lovely soft water of our forest cabin, I was absolutely blown away by how gorgeous it felt afterward. It really was softer and shinier and even had more volume. It felt clean and pleasant, and I felt well groomed with it on my head.

If I'd have been able to stay there, all would have been well. Sadly when we came back to our hard water home, my hair became a little greasy again. Just enough so that it never felt exactly clean.

I tried adding a cider vinegar rinse to my washing—basically washing my hair in warm water, and then adding cider vinegar to a jug of water and tipping that over my head to finish.

It did help, a little. But cider vinegar is expensive! I was using a bottle of cider vinegar every week—and okay, I made sure to get the glass ones, so I wasn't using plastic. But it still seemed expensive, and wasteful, and I was tired of my hair never feeling entirely clean.

So when a shop opened up nearby where you could take your own containers and refill them with shampoo and conditioner, I caved and went back onto the shampoo and conditioner regime.

If you're lucky enough to live in a soft water area, I would give this a try, though. There is an immense feeling of liberation in the knowledge that you don't need these chemicals to live, and that your own body is capable of keeping itself presentable if you let it.

If you live in a hard water area too, I would still give it a try. It might suit you, and as I say, immense feelings of liberation and bodily reconciliation are to be had for the experiment.

Dry shampoo and talc

Both of these are so easy to make yourself that it hardly qualifies as a recipe. Basically, take some cornflour (aka cornstarch if you are from the US). Add a couple of drops of essential oil for scent and shake to distribute the oil. Hey presto, dry shampoo powder, or talc.

To use as dry shampoo, apply the powder to the roots of your hair using a shaving brush or a blusher brush. Let it sit for a while then brush out vigorously—your hair is now no longer greasy.

To use as talc, use as talc.

Toothpaste and Toothbrushes

When I started going plastic free, there was only one alternative to plastic toothbrushes, and that was the Humble Brush[32], which has a bamboo handle and nylon bristles, and comes in biodegradable packaging. The Humble Co also do toothpaste tabs in a glass jar, so that's one stop for all your dental needs.

Alternatively, there are other brands out there. Here's Cosmopolitan's review of five different bamboo toothbrushes[33]. The Olas looks interesting, with its natural bristles, but £8 is a bit pricey.

---

32.   https://www.thehumble.co/collections/humble-brush

33.   https://www.cosmopolitan.com/style-beauty/beauty/g30927968/
         best-bamboo-eco-friendly-toothbrushes/

Likewise you can google for eco-friendly toothpastes and you will get a list something like this[34]. There are a lot of toothpaste tabs in glass jars available, or in bio-degradable pouches.

You may find you're perfectly fine with toothpaste tabs. I, sadly, have sensitive teeth, and if I don't use enamel repair toothpaste on them, within about a week I have such awful toothache and headache that my life is not worth living. I am therefore stuck with Sensodyne toothpaste, which comes in a plastic tube.

Fortunately, my dentist takes these in for specialist recycling, so it's not as bad as it could be. But I would totally be on the tabs if I could!

Liquid soap

Liquid soap is generally bought in little plastic pump bottles, which we don't want to be regularly buying and throwing out if we can help it.

One solution to this is really simple—just use solid soap. There are lots of places where you can buy hand made artisanal soap and support a local craftperson. Hand made soap from locally sourced ingredients made by a local artist is the tip top gold standard of sustainability. The Little Soap Company, for example do an Eco Warrior range of plastic free soaps.[35]

If that's not available, you can also buy hard soap wrapped in paper at the supermarket.

My husband is the liquid soap fan in the family and I must admit to being baffled at why it's so superior to the solid version. But that may be because I have my own private bar of soap and don't have to share it with anyone. I acknowledge that there's something quite icky about a damp, dirty piece of oft-used hard soap in a public bathroom.

So perhaps liquid soap is a thing after all.

One solution to the liquid soap problem is that you can change your hard soap into liquid soap, if you dissolve it in a pan of hot water.

---

34.   https://www.sustainablejungle.com/best-of-sustainable-beauty/zero-waste-toothpaste/

35.   https://www.littlesoapcompany.co.uk/

Take a 4oz bar of hard soap, grate it into a pan of 4 pints of water, heat and stir until it dissolves.

Cool. Give it a good whip with a hand whisk to even out any lumps. Then pour into an empty pump dispenser. Hey presto, liquid soap.

Alternatively, you can buy eco-friendly liquid soap. These[36] all claim to be eco-friendly, but frustratingly do not fess up to what their containers are made of. I've been fooled many times into thinking packaging was glass from the picture and then having it turn up and be plastic. Even Ecover lets me down here, although you can buy a 5L Ecover bottle[37] and refill your individual containers from it.

Fill, however, do a liquid soap in a glass bottle here,[38] which is probably your best bet if you don't make your own.

Cosmetics, cosmetic wipes

I can't speak about cosmetics, since I've never worn them. A quick google brings up Zao's Essence of Nature[39] range, which is sold in bamboo containers you buy only once, refilling them as necessary. But I'm sure that if makeup interests you, the process of discovering your own preferred brands will be a pleasure for you.

I am, however, going to take the chance to say, "You really don't need any of them, you know! Imagine how much money you could save and how much waste you could avoid if you just stopped wearing cosmetics right now. Your pocket, nature and your skin would thank you for it."

Cosmetic wipes?

---

36.   https://www.ethicalsuperstore.com/category/beauty-health-and-wellbeing/
        bath-and-body/hand-soap/eco-friendly.htm

37.   https://www.ecoverdirect.com/products/hand-soap-5l/
        ehandsoap5l.aspx?productid=ehandsoap5l

38.   https://www.fillrefill.co/product/hand-soap-500ml/

39.   https://zaoessenceofnature.co.uk

I think you can guess what I'm going to say here, after experiencing my stance on other kinds of wipes and sheets. You really don't need them. An old-fashioned face cloth will do the job just fine.

"But what if I'm outside somewhere—at a festival or something—and I want to pull a cleansing wipe out of my bag, somewhere where I don't have access to soap and water?"

In that case you can buy (or make) reusable cotton pads like these that I found on Ebay[40]. They're easy to make by stitching some cotton terry fabric to a patterned cotton back, but—given the price of fabric—they may be just as cheap to buy.

Soak the reusable pads in a very mild soap and water solution and put them in a waterproof container, such as a washbag or a takeaway container. That can go in your bag as though it was a pack of wipes.

Alternatively, if you're currently using the kind of tough baby-wipes that are full of plastic fibers to stop them from tearing, then you can prevent waste by reusing them. Put them in the washing machine with your normal load—they survive this treatment just fine—and then put *them* into a waterproof container with a mild soap and water solution. If you keep re-using the same pack of wipes, they never become waste!

Shaving kit

I don't know about you, but for shaving purposes, I used to regularly buy a multi-pack of disposable Bic razors. Everything except the actual razor blades was plastic and they came in a plastic bag.

Even if you're not quite as bad as this, the chances are that you're using a multi-bladed razor with a plastic body, along with shaving cream in a plastic tube or tub, or in an aerosol can. If you use a shaving brush, you may already have a wood or ceramic handled one with boar's

---

40.   https://www.ebay.co.uk/i/
274226572131?rt=nc&_trkparms=aid%3D1110001%26algo%3DSPLICE.SIM%26ao%3D2
%26asc%3D20160908110712%26meid%3Ded9846e310e14a2f8959cf1c9c74b2e0%26pid%3
D100677%26rk%3D5%26rkt%3D30%26mehot%3Dnone%26sd%3D274226589771%26itm
%3D274226572131%26pmt%3D0%26noa%3D1%26pg%3D2386202%26algv%3DDefault

bristles, but if you have a plastic handled one, consider replacing it with something biodegradable when next you need a new one.

The nice thing about going plastic free as far as shaving goes, is that this is another opportunity to buy yourself something new.

Have a google for 'Plastic Free Safety Razor' and you'll find a plethora of options for all metal, or metal and wood razor bodies. You then buy a tube of loose razor blades like this,[41] and when the razor gets blunt, you simply replace the blade.

Gillette do a razor blade recycling scheme[42] to which you can send the blunt blades to close the loop perfectly, or alternatively they can be sealed inside some other metal container (like a squashed can) and sent to your normal recycling, which is much better at dealing with metal than plastic.

When I was first going through this process, the hardest thing was to find shaving soap that didn't come in a plastic container, but since then that has become much easier and a search for 'Plastic free shaving soap'[43] turns up any number of options.

Deodorant

The great majority of shop-bought deodorants come in a plastic container, but there are alternatives out there. One is to buy a commercial product that comes in a cardboard tube, or a solid bar, or as a cream in a tin such as one of these.[44] I can recommend the Lush Aromaco Solid Deodorant, which works really well and smells gorgeous.

Alternatively, you can make your own:

Liquid deodorant which you can put into a roll on deodorant container[45].

---

41.   https://www.amazon.co.uk/100-Astra-Superior-Platinum-Shaving/dp/B00CK7NQ8Y

42.   https://www.gillette.co.uk/recycle.list

43.   https://www.amazon.co.uk/

        s?k=plastic+free+shaving+soap&i=drugstore&ref=nb_sb_noss_1

44.   https://naturaler.co.uk/best-plastic-free-deodorant-uk/

- 25mls milk of magnesia
- 25mls witch hazel
- 1tsp bicarbonate of soda
- 12 drops essential oil of choice

Combine all the ingredients and stir until the bicarb dissolves. Pour into your roll on bottle and cap.

It may need shaking a little before you use it. I've used this for over a year now and found it very effective. I much prefer the smell to the rather artificial smells of commercial deodorants. The witch hazel tightens the pores so it also has a slight antiperspirant effect, but it does tend to leave white marks.

Menstrual Products

"Did you know that conventional sanitary pads contain a high percentage of plastic? One estimate is that pads are made of up to 90% plastic [46] *– another is that a pack of menstrual pads is equivalent to 4 plastic bags* [47].

Tampons have plastic in them too – even in the string – and plastic applicators are made from polyethylene (PE) and polypropylene (PP).... The average person who menstruates throws away up to 200 kg of menstrual products [48] in their lifetime.*"

- Friends of the Earth

That's not good, is it? In addition, pads can be made of rayon (aka viscose) the production of which releases tonnes of toxic chemicals into the environment. This is a place where you can make a huge difference to the environment almost at once.

Your options for plastic free menstrual products are:

45.   https://www.amazon.co.uk/gp/product/B07FQ2P8ZZ

46.   https://www.natracare.com/why-natracare/plastic-free/

47.   https://www.natracare.com/blog/turning-the-tide-on-plastic-period-waste/

48.   https://www.london.gov.uk/sites/default/files/
         plastics_unflushables_-_submited_evidence.pdf

1. The moon cup[49]

The moon cup is a little silicone cup that you essentially stick up your vagina and which collects the blood before it can exit your body. You take it out every 4-8 hours and empty the contents down the toilet. Then you rinse it out and put it back for another 4-8 hours.

Moon cups cost around £21 for the name brand ones, and can be as little as £12 for copy cats from other makers. As you only need to buy one of them you will soon start to save money now you never have to buy tampons or pads again.

I've tried this, and it takes a bit of getting used to. They warn you on the website that you might take two or three periods to really get the knack of it, and that's the literal truth. But I found that once I did get used to it, I wished I'd had access to it years ago. It's so much simpler, less messy, less smelly and less prone to embarrassing leakage than pads, and so much less at risk of toxic shock than tampons.

2. Reusable pads

Instead of buying disposable pads every month, you could make or buy a set of fabric pads which you can wash and re-use. A set of pads to buy can be quite an investment, as each pad can cost around £10. But of course, as they're reusable, they can last a long time. You can find a wide variety of sizes and absorbencies here on Honour Your Flow,[50] or if you know what you're looking for, try on Ebay[51], which gives you a baffling amount of choice and is considerably cheaper.

If you're looking to make your own, there are a number of tutorials and sewing patterns available on the internet, such as this one by Red & Honey[52], or this one by WikiHow[53].

---

49.   https://www.mooncup.co.uk/

50.   https://www.honouryourflow.co.uk/

51.   https://www.ebay.co.uk/sch/
          i.html?_from=R40&_trksid=p2380057.m570.l1311.R1.TR9.TRC2.A0.H0.Xreusable+menstr.
          TRS0&_nkw=reusable+menstrual+pads&_sacat=0

52.   https://redandhoney.com/make-your-own-cloth-menstrual-pads/

3. Menstrual underwear

Menstrual underwear is a mystery to me in terms of how it works. I assume it's just like pants that have reusable padding sewn into them, but if that's so the layers seem to be impressively thin. This is the most expensive of the options, with five pairs of pants coming to over £100, but if it works just think of the freedom! I'd be giddy with it.

Post unexpected hysterectomy, this is no longer something I can test, so I'll just drop a website link on you and leave it up to you to investigate. Good Housekeeping have done a piece on the 7 best types of period underwear here[54].

That's about it for the bathroom, I think. Now let's tackle somewhere even more difficult... the heart of the home, the kitchen.

---

53.   https://www.wikihow.com/Make-Your-Own-Reusable-Menstrual-Pads

54.   https://www.goodhousekeeping.com/health-products/g27421796/best-period-panties/

Kitchen

GROCERIES

The Kitchen is a big nexus of plastic use, which is why this chapter is one of the last. Once you've got rid of plastic from the rest of the house, you'll be a pro, and the kitchen will not be so daunting.

One of the big things we do in the kitchen is cook, so let's start out with food. Now your eyes have been opened to the problem of plastic, you'll notice that almost every bit of food that comes into your house comes wrapped in plastic.

Cereal boxes have a plastic inner liner. Meat comes in a plastic tray, sealed with plastic wrap. Yoghurts come in plastic pots. Multipacks of tins come shrink-wrapped in plastic. Milk and soft drinks come in plastic bottles. Vegetables come in plastic punnets. The sandwiches you buy for lunch have a plastic viewing window. Even your salads come in plastic boxes or bags. And all of this is single-use plastic. If you're lucky it may claim that it's recyclable. If not, this is straight-in-the-bin-into-landfill-and-oceans plastic of the sort that we most want to never have to produce again.

So what can we do about de-plasticking our groceries?

Fruit and Veg

Let's start by buying our fruit and veg from places where we can get them loose, in no packaging at all. That's what we're carrying our fabric bags for in our shopping kit, after all. Even from the supermarket this is possible for a lot of items, like onions, baking potatoes and mushrooms. If your supermarket doesn't sell a particular fruit or vegetable loose, there is usually a market in town with stalls who will. If you're lucky there may be a local greengrocer or a farm shop instead, where you can simultaneously buy plastic-free *and* support local farmers, eliminating extra waste and petrol spent on the supermarket's long supply chain.

Another easy fix is to eschew any multipack that comes with a plastic outer wrapper. Just buy however many items you want separately. If you're a big user of social media, you could drop your supermarket a quick message saying "Not buying multipacks from you any more until they come bound together with cardboard instead of plastic." If other people are also avoiding the egregious plastic, the supermarket may have noticed a decline in sales, and may well consider taking your suggestion on.

Onto more difficult items:

Meat

As we said last chapter, rather than buy your meat in plastic trays, you can instead go to the supermarket's deli counter and ask for them to cut you the amount you want and put it into the reusable containers you're carrying. This goes for sausages, bacon, cured meats etc too.

We are lucky enough to have a very well regarded butcher in our town, so I make a special trip there for meat. They're always happy to let me use my own containers, and I'm happy to support a local small business which knows exactly where its animals have come from and how well they're treated.

Cheese

Cheese is another thing that you can get from the deli counter, cut to fit your own container. It sadly means that you have much less choice than you would down the cheese aisle, especially if you can't really afford to buy any of those fancy wax-wrapped cheeses that look so lovely but are so small. But needs must...

Butter, fortunately, you can always find wrapped in wax paper.

Milk

I don't think you can do better for milk than to find your own milk-man, who will deliver it to your door in glass bottles, take the bottles away again when they're empty, and re-use them over and over. This is good for your environment, good for local dairies and good for you, whose milk turns up as if by magic with no effort from you at all.

You can find a milkman near you by putting your postcode in the search box on this site.[55]

Yoghurt

As a non-vegan vegetarian, I am a huge yoghurt-eater. I have it with my breakfast and put it in my dinner, and frequently eat it as a snack. Unfortunately there seem to be no commercially available yoghurts that don't come in a plastic pot.

It's possible that you don't eat yoghurt at all. If so, you don't have a problem! If you eat yoghurt only very rarely, you also don't have much of a problem - just stop using it the rare times that you would and congratulate yourself that it doesn't make much of a difference to you.

If, however, you also eat an awful lot of yoghurt and can't do without it, I can only really suggest that you try making your own. Buy yourself a little, inexpensive yoghurt maker (you can do it without, using a thermos flask, but it's more difficult and more prone to spoiling) and order extra milk from the milkman instead.

To make yoghurt:

Heat up two pints of milk in a saucepan until the milk boils.

Remove from heat immediately, cover the pan with a lid and set the pan in a cool place for the milk to cool down. You want the milk to reach 43 degrees Centigrade.

---

55.   https://findmeamilkman.net/

In my experience, it will take the milk at least two hours to cool. It doesn't matter if the milk cools *below* 43 degrees because the yoghurt maker will reheat it anyway. If you forget the pan out there and rediscover it four hours later when the milk is barely tepid, don't worry too much.

Buy yourself an heirloom yoghurt starter from the internet. An heirloom yoghurt starter is one which will not die or give weird results after two or three batches. As long as you wash all your equipment well, an heirloom yoghurt starter will let you continue making new batches from it for months.

Put your milk and your yoghurt starter together into the jug of the yoghurt maker, give it a stir, and set your yoghurt maker going. It'll usually take 10-12 hours, so I put it on overnight.

In the morning, you'll have a pot full of yoghurt and whey. The whey—a thin, yellow liquid—can be used to feed your acid-loving plants. Your lawn will love it!

Take out enough of the yoghurt to start the next batch and reserve this in a small air-tight pot in the fridge.

Now you can whip the rest of the yoghurt until it's smooth, and store it in a Kilner jar (or the equivalent) until you come to eat it.

If you go the way of making your own yoghurt, the first few times you do it, you'll be hovering over the milk pan as it heats, anxious not to let it boil over. You'll check the temperature every five minutes as it cools, thinking, 'it must be ready by now!' You'll be anxiously waiting for the end of the cooking time, ready to decant it immediately into cleaned jars. And you'll think, 'my God, this is such a performance! It takes so long! I can't be doing this every other day.'

Fortunately, as you get more used to the process, you learn that it doesn't need to be kept under such strict surveillance. Heat the milk as you make your breakfast, and you'll be able to hear when it's just about to boil. Then stick it somewhere cool and forget about it for at least two hours. When lunch time comes around, the milk will probably be ready to go in the yoghurt maker with the reserved starter. You'll get to know to tell it's the right temperature by touch rather than by needing a thermometer (though a thermometer is essential to start off with.)

Then you put it on for 10 hours and forget about it again, until it's ready to decant the following morning just before breakfast. My point being that once you get used to it, it doesn't feel like its any trouble any more.

I do miss flavoured yoghurts, but it's possible to flavour your own, by mixing in some hot-chocolate powder, for example, or a spoonful of those syrups with which you flavour coffee, or by blitzing in a handful of fruit. And the truth is that your own live yoghurt is much, much better for you than the dead, artificially flavoured store-bought version any time.

Starches (Pasta, rice, oats, cous-cous etc)

Grains in supermarkets also tend to come in 1kg plastic bags. In our household, we use a bag of regular pasta, a bag of gluten-free pasta and a bag of rice every week, and a bag of cous-cous every one and a half weeks. That's roughly four single-use plastic bags to throw out every week, or two hundred and eight plastic bags in the rubbish every year. Many of which will end up in the sea.

We don't want that!

Fortunately in a lot of areas you can now find dry-goods stores which will sell you these things loose too. In Ely, I make a weekly visit to The Prospects Trust, where they have dispensers full of loose pasta, rice, muesli, cous-cous, lentils, dry split peas, oats etc where I can fill up a bag I bring with me from home.

Look around your area, and you may find you have one of these shops close by too.

If there is no such shop near you, then there are probably lots of other people like you, wishing that there was. See if you can start a bulk buying cooperative on Facebook or other social media site. Then you can pool money, buy from bulk suppliers, and at least minimize the amount of plastic you use.

Bread

We are fortunate enough to have a local farm shop which sells bread made by a local baker. The bread comes wrapped in paper and unsliced, but is a little pricey. We don't mind because we need gluten free, and the shop does that. If you don't need gluten free, however, many supermarkets now have an in-store bakery from which you can get an unwrapped loaf for which you can take your own bag.

Fortunately eggs come in cardboard and sugar comes in paper. You don't need to worry about cans. Like glass, metal can be very successfully recycled. As for other things that I haven't mentioned here, I can only say "'try to find a plastic-free product. If that isn't currently possible, perhaps write to the manufacturer asking when a plastic-free version will be available, and consider whether you actually need that thing at all.' Once you've done that, you've done everything you reasonably can do, even if the answer is 'yes. I need that thing.'"

Cleaning Products

If you're like me, the cupboard under your sink in the kitchen is stocked full of cleaning products. I used to have floor cleaning liquid (in a plastic bottle), washing up liquid (in a plastic bottle), kitchen cleaner, bathroom cleaner, glass cleaner, oven cleaner, bleach, all in plastic bottles, along with an assortment of mould remover, grout cleaner and lime-scale remover—especially that blue stuff that you pour down the toilet.

That amounts to a heck of a lot of plastic bottles (spray or otherwise,) one or two of which I was throwing away every week.

For my first pass on tackling these, I looked up "how to make your own cleaning products," on the internet. I found a plethora of recipes, some of which could never have worked. (You can't put soap and vinegar together—the soap separates out into its component parts.)

I narrowed these down to (a) a surface cleaner, and (b) a limescale remover for cleaning glass and disinfecting ceramic/porcelain surfaces, particularly in the bathroom.

Glass/Bathroom cleaner

Dilute spirit vinegar with an equal volume of boiled water.

For the glass/bathroom cleaner I didn't find anything better than spirit vinegar—the white, highly distilled vinegar that looks like water. This is so effective that you can dilute it 1:1 with water, put it in a spray bottle, and it will still take the water-marks off your glassware, and dissolve the limescale from your toilet bowl.

I bought myself a set of three glass bottles with spray nozzles, and filled one of them with this diluted vinegar mix, slapped a pretty label on it and I was ready to never buy spray bathroom cleaner, or toilet-duck, or any of those clean-up-under-the-rim toxic bright blue concoctions again. That was nearly a year ago, and my toilets are just as clean as they always have been, if not a bit more so.

My daughter absolutely swears by this stuff, which she thinks is miraculous. I wouldn't go that far, but I think it's certainly no worse than the commercial sprays.

Just make sure that you buy the spirit vinegar in a glass bottle, and you're sorted!

Kitchen cleaner/Dirt lifter

Makes 500ml:

100ml of pure Castille liquid soap

2 TBSP bicarbonate of soda (aka sodium bicarbonate.)

400ml boiled water

10 drops of essential oil of choice.

(I use essential oils which have been proved to have disinfectant qualities, like lavender, peppermint and tea-tree oil.)

Mix all together until the bicarb dissolves in the water. Put in a spray bottle and use instead of commercial spray cleaner.

This stuff *I* consider pretty miraculous. The bicarb gives it a dirt lifting effect similar to what you get from those fancy foaming sprays that claim to be full of oxygen. Spray the most baked on dirt, leave it for a little while to work, and wipe off again. Hey presto! It tackles oil and baked on food better than any commercial spray I've ever used.

Because you can blend your own scent, it smells much better than the commercial sprays. And because all it contains is soap and bicarb, you can be reassured that it's a good deal better for your health than the mixes of unknown chemicals that you used to spray on everything from those neon colored bottles.

The one disadvantage of this spray is that if you don't wipe it off again thoroughly, it will leave a white residue of bicarbonate of soda behind. But I'm not sure this is such a bad thing. If you see a white residue, just wipe it off with clean water and a cloth. Then you can be certain that the surface underneath is so clean that not even the cleaning product is left.

Obviously, I'm a convert to the making of my own cleaning fluids. It's easy and cheap, and so am I!

But if you do not want to go to so much trouble, there's always Fill[56], with their glass bottles again. They're much more expensive than making your own, but they're less rustic and even less trouble.

Washing up liquid. Floor cleaning liquid.

Both of these I generally get from Ecover, because they're eco-friendly and non-toxic to the environment. As I regularly water my garden with my used washing-up water, I can attest to the fact that none of my plants have been damaged by this detergent.

As I said, I am fortunate enough to live near a town where there is a hardware shop which stocks refills for Ecover products. You can Find your Local Refill Station[57] here.

What if you don't have a store like this, though?

---

56.   https://www.fillrefill.co/

57.   https://www.ecover.com/store-locator/

Well, then you can just buy your own bulk containers from Ecover[58]. Put them on top of your fridge or under your sink and refill your bottles from there. Maybe you could share the cost among you and your neighbors, and become a refill station yourself. It's a good way to start spreading the plastic-free message wherever you live.

You can also find washing up liquid and floor cleaning liquid from Fill.[59] Or if neither option appeals, you can find alternatives on The Ethical Superstore[60].

A NOTE ON FLOOR CLEANING. You've probably seen the adverts for a snazzy new floor mop which involves a wipe that attaches to the mop-head which you use once and throw away. I haven't actually looked at the thing, because the sheer wastefulness of the concept is so blatant I didn't feel I needed to, but I'm prepared to bet a lot of money that the 'disposable' wipes involved in this system are strengthened with plastic. Yet another place where you're being encouraged to create an endless stream of non-biodegradable toxic garbage which you then have to buy more of every month.

Needless to say, if you're trying to cut down on plastic use, it's better to have an old fashioned mop and bucket with a wringer, which you buy once and then use for years and years without having to pay for additional stuff that you're going to throw away at an unnecessary drain on both the environment and your bank balance.

Now that I've become aware of this stuff, it is shocking to me how much we are encouraged to buy more and more things to immediately throw away. It makes sense for the people who make such things to want us to continue buying them, but it doesn't make sense for us to

---

58.   https://www.ecoverdirect.com/departments/refills.aspx?deptid=RF

59.   https://www.fillrefill.co/

60.   https://www.ethicalsuperstore.com/

capitulate to being exploited for profit in such a way, at such a cost to ourselves and the environment.

What about dishwasher tablets?

Both Fill[61] and Ecover[62] have dishwasher powder instead of those brightly coloured, poisonous, plastic-wrapped capsules.

Other kinds of scrap plastic packaging
Clingfilm

Clingfilm is very useful for wrapping your sandwiches and storing your food in the fridge, but it's also the epitome of the kind of plastic that you use once and then throw away. Fortunately there are alternatives.

I'm sure you've heard about beeswax wraps by now—these are sheets of fabric which have been permeated with food-grade beeswax. The wax means that the fabric is now waterproof and air-proof just like clingfilm. It also means that you can bend the stiff fabric into shape around whatever you're containing, and it will stay there.

I'm quite a fan of beeswax wraps, but it's largely because I make my own. The ones you get in the shops are ridiculously expensive.

HOW TO MAKE BEESWAX wraps

1. Cut a piece of cotton into a size you think is suitable. You don't have to hem them, as the wax will prevent fraying. I have mostly 14" square wraps, but shops sell them smaller than that, and a couple of 10" ones might be useful. The nice thing about making them yourself is you can make whatever size suits you best.

2. Lay the sheet of cotton on top of a piece of greaseproof paper

61.   https://www.fillrefill.co

62.   https://www.ecoverdirect.com/
          search.aspx?q=all-in-one%20dishwasher%20tablets%20-%2022

on your ironing board.

3. Using a cheese-grater, grate a solid piece of beeswax over the surface of the cotton until the fabric is lightly covered with bits of wax.
4. Put another piece of greaseproof paper on top of that.
5. Iron over the top of the greaseproof paper until the wax melts. Then give it another few passes with the iron to spread the melted wax and allow it to permeate the fabric evenly.
6. Peel the greaseproof paper apart and set the wax-soaked fabric on a flat surface to cool and harden.
7. You can now use the same greaseproof paper to make however many more wraps you have fabric and wax for.

Some commercial wax wraps contain resin to give them stickiness, so that they will stick to themselves and to the surfaces of other vessels, like bowls. I personally don't like the stickiness, which makes them icky to handle and tricky to wash. With plain wax ones, the fabric can simply be made malleable by the heat of your hands enough to be shaped around the bowls. Then it will set in place when you leave it.

Plain wax wraps can easily be re-melted and refreshed if they get creased—just repeat the whole 'ironing through greaseproof paper' thing.

I store my wax wraps rolled loosely around the rolling pin, and clean them gently with cool soapy water followed by vinegar-and-water after use.

EVEN ONCE YOU'VE SORTED out these big items, you'd be amazed how much plastic waste is left.

If you're not convinced that you generate much waste, try going zero waste for a month. Tell yourself that you must throw out nothing. You can put stuff in the recycling bins (as long as it's only the stuff the recycling authority allows.) If you have a compost pile, you can put stuff in the compost pile. You can take good quality items you don't want to the charity shops to be re-sold. (Or you can re-sell them yourself on Shpock or Ebay.) But nothing must go in the waste bin. Nothing must be put out for the bin men.

Very soon after you try this, things will begin piling up.

What kind of things? Well, do you eat biscuits that come with plastic wrappers? Those plastic wrappers are now your problem. What about the inside sleeves of cereal packets? What about the stiff, shiny transparent plastic that goes across the windows of letters and is inset into the paper bags the supermarket puts bread in? What about crisp packets? What about the bubble-wrap that comes when you order parcels online?

Your own pile of scrap plastic will depend on what you regularly eat or buy, and what you've already managed to cut out earlier in this chapter. But you'll be amazed and dismayed by how much of it there still is.

Terracycle

This is where Terracycle[63] comes in.

Terracycle is a scheme which partners with the producers of nasty plastic packaging to post that nasty packaging back to them to be recycled. It works on the customers' end by means of volunteers.

Someone decides to set up a local recycling station—ie a couple of big boxes in their garage where they will store their own and other people's waste plastic until there is enough to box up and send to the Terracycle collection point. The person who runs the recycling station earns a little bit of cash for their favourite charity for doing it, and the waste is shipped off to the manufacturer to be dealt with.

Currently, Terracycle has collection points for biscuit wrappers, crisp bags, used water filters, packaging from cleaning and laundry

---

products, contact lenses, Flash wipes, rubber gloves, Pringles cans and many more items.

Go to the Terracycle website to see the full list and search for a collection point near you. If there isn't a local collection point for that thing, you can consider whether you'd like to become one. They will help you with that.

Recycling

"There are limited facilities to recycle plastic in the UK. A lot of money is demanded to separate and recycle different types of plastic using specialist machines. While money is needed to recycle, money is also made by recycling, making it the preferred waste management method. Local councils in the UK collect recycled waste from green bins and kerbside schemes but don't accept all types of plastic. Which plastics are recycled depends on the facilities local councils have available. Meaning what's recyclable in one area, might not be in another.

That's why over half of our plastic ends up in landfill or incineration. This is an expensive disposal method that doesn't give as much back to the economy as recycling. With limited capacity for recycling millions of tonnes of waste in the UK, the government ships waste overseas to countries including Malaysia, China and India. This helps the government hit management targets but doesn't actually dispose of the waste." - ProEnvironmental Recycling Solutions[64]

Once we've gone through the Terracycle options, there should be only the most difficult items left to get rid of in an eco-friendly way. We're now down to things like clingfilm, bubble-wrap, the insides of cereal packets and that very clear crinkly plastic you get in the windows of letters and packaging to let you see what's inside.

Unfortunately, unlike glass and tin cans, plastic is just one of those things that our current recycling system is not very good with. That's why recycling is all the way down here in my list of how to deal with

---

the last smidgen of plastic that you just can't avoid buying. It's here as a last resort, after you've simply stopped buying as much plastic as you possibly can, rather than a first resort.

Nevertheless, it's still a step above just throwing the waste plastic in the bin. If you don't know what else to do with your plastic wrap/film, there's a simple test to see if it is recyclable or not. Put your thumb against it and push. If the plastic film is stretchy, then it's recyclable. If it isn't, it isn't.

Bubble-wrap is stretchy, and so are the the inner bags from cereal packs. So these can go along with any plastic bags that you might be sending back to plastic bag recycling. (Ie, you can put them in the plastic bag recycling bins at supermarkets, or give them to your delivery driver when you're getting a supermarket delivery to be taken back to the supermarket and put in their recycling pile.

Ecobricks[65]

So now we're left with a pile of miscellaneous plastic film. The kind of stuff you get wrapped around items you've bought online—the crinkly cellophane in which tombola prizes and bunches of flowers are wrapped, and the plastic windows people seem to think we need in bags and packaging to see what's inside.

This non-stretchy stuff is not currently recyclable *anywhere*.

The best thing we can do with this stuff is to confine it somewhere where it takes up the least amount of space and does not get out to choke a bird or abrade into tiny micro-particles and poison the sea-bed further in the watercycle. For this, we can make ecobricks[66].

Basically, take an empty plastic bottle, such as a 600ml bottle that once contained bottled water, or a 1.5L bottle that once contained a fizzy drink. Wash it out, and then fill it with all that plastic that couldn't go anywhere else. (Both the bottle and the plastic have to be washed and dried first.)

---

65.   https://www.ecobricks.org/

66.   https://www.ecobricks.org/

With a bit of elbow grease, you can pack almost 600g of plastic wrap into a 1.5L bottle, and as plastic wrap is so light, you wouldn't believe how much of it that is.

Eventually, once you've filled enough bottles, you can use them as the 'brick' part of a building. Lay them on top of each other and mortar in the gaps, and you can build yourself a barbeque or a garden seat. Alternatively, you can validate your ecobrick on the ecobricks site[67] (a process of making sure it's packed tightly enough so that it is the right weight per volume. Then you can send your validated ecobrick to any community project that might be collecting them nearby.

This is not as easy as it sounds. I definitely recommend going on the ecobrick website and watching their instruction videos on how to correctly pack the plastic in. You won't believe how much of it you can get rid of this way, and if you've had it piling up on the side for a few months you also won't believe what a relief it is to have it contained and managed. The garden furniture which you can build with it afterward is just a bonus.

I think we're getting to the end of the kitchen now.

To summarize:

- Meat and cheese - from the deli counter in your own container
- Fruit and veg - loose from supermarket or market in your own bag
- Grains and pasta - loose from bulk buy shop in your own bag
- Bread - from the bakery, unwrapped or in paper bag
- Milk - from milkman in reusable glass bottles
- Yoghurt - make your own from the above milk
- Cleaning products - make your own or refills from Ecover or Fill

---

67.   https://www.ecobricks.org/

- Various kinds of small plastic products - Terracycle
- Plastic film - carrier bag recycling or Ecobrick

It sounds daunting, but it's not really that bad. And you'll be so proud when you first realize that you haven't put the bin out for months. The world will thank you, and so do I!

Bedroom, aka clothing

YOU KNOW HOW, IN THE laundry chapter, I mentioned that dryer sheets were made with polyester fibers to strengthen them? And I mentioned that polyester shed little microfibers of plastic into the environment, especially during the washing and drying process? I think you can guess where I'm going with this...

Even invisible plastic waste is toxic to the environment.

"New studies show that alarming numbers of tiny fibers from synthetic fabrics are making their way from your washing machine into aquatic animals," says the Guardian in this article[68]. *"These microfibers then travel to your local wastewater treatment plant, where up to 40% of them enter rivers, lakes and oceans," according to findings published on the researchers' website. Synthetic microfibers are particularly dangerous because they have the potential to poison the food chain. The fibers' size also allows them to be readily consumed by fish and other wildlife. These plastic fibers have the potential to bioaccumulate, concentrating toxins in the bodies of larger animals, higher up the food chain."*

---

68.   https://www.theguardian.com/environment/2016/jun/20/
microfibers-plastic-pollution-oceans-patagonia-synthetic-clothes-microbeads

"Microfiber pollution[69] is taking an incredible toll on our natural ecosystems and causing untold damage" says Ecosource.net[70] *"It is important to note when referring to microfiber pollution, it is not specifically addressing the standard household "microfiber cloth" which is usually created from a blend of polyester and polyamide or nylon (which means it is made from plastic), but in fact the microscopic fiber residue that is left behind when using or washing synthetic fabrics."*

So clothes that contain synthetic/man-made fabrics are poisoning the environment with tiny, invisible particles of plastic, which will not biodegrade and will hang around for centuries killing fish, accumulating toxins and getting into our own food.

As if that wasn't bad enough, the use of fossil fuels to make those fabrics in the first place emits so much $CO2$ that the fashion industry is one of the worst culprits in causing climate change!

"Relatively cheap and easily available, polyester is now used in about 60% of our clothes. But, if we take into account the fossil fuels used in its production, $CO2$ emissions for polyester clothing are nearly three times higher than for cotton! Our reliance on polyester is one of the reasons why the fashion industry is one of the most polluting industries in the world; both in terms of its emissions-heavy production and the non-biodegradable waste it leaves behind," says Greenpeace.[71]

What this means is that—unexpectedly—your clothes are a big part of the problem of plastic.

That's just so unfair, isn't it? That's why I left this chapter to the last in our jaunt around the house. For me, at least, the prospect of changing my entire wardrobe, and the very sheets on my bed, was perhaps the most daunting part of trying to minimize my damage to

69.   https://www.ecosourcellc.net/2019/05/06/microfiber-pollution-is-a-real-thing/

70.   https://www.ecosourcellc.net/2019/08/08/
       microfiber-pollution-and-the-environment-what-is-it-and-how-do-we-stop-it/

71.   https://www.greenpeace.org/international/story/6956/
       what-are-microfibers-and-why-are-our-clothes-polluting-the-oceans/

the environment. I thought you might like to work up to it by doing the other rooms first.

So, what can we do about clothes made from plastic?

Since the production, use and disposal of clothes made from synthetic fibers is bad, and we want to encourage companies to make fully natural, biodegradable clothes, the first thing we can do is to decide only to buy clothes made from natural fabrics in future.

That means wool, cotton, hemp, bamboo, silk, linen, leather and jute.

(I'll discuss rayon aka viscose in a later chapter, but suffice it to say although viscose is not made of plastic, it has its own problems.

If you already have viscose garments, however, at least you don't need to worry about those shedding plastic microfibers, and they can be washed and dried in with the natural fiber clothing.)

"Alex! Do you know how much pure wool, cotton, bamboo, silk, hemp, linen and leather clothes cost!! Do you think I'm made of money?"

It's a problem, isn't it? I have to admit, I like to go out shopping and come home with a new piece of clothing. Buying yourself a new dress or shirt as a treat is one of those minor luxuries that make life worth living—like cake from a coffee shop. But I've got so used to fast fashion, to clothes that cost a tenner or less, where I can buy them without thinking and not worry when they tear in two months time, that the prospect of paying for quality items that were grown in sustainable ways boggles my mind.

I'm not made of money either.

Unfortunately there's no getting round this problem. We've grown accustomed to buying clothes for far less money than they are worth. In the fast fashion business, we've created an industry which is pillaging and polluting the earth, is reliant on child labour and the oppression of developing countries, is ruining ecosystems and contributing to global warming. There is no hack to get round this. It's one of those sticking points where we will just have to learn to consume less so that we can consume better. More on that later.

Since you and I are ahead of the curve, there is however a way in which we can still shop affordably while also treating ourselves to good quality garments made from natural fibers. This is to buy second hand.

Eventually, fossil fuels will be exhausted and cheap clothes will become unobtainable, at which point even things in the charity shop will become serious purchases we will have to worry about. For now, however, we have a good opportunity to get a jump on the competition and buy a good wardrobe on the cheap by buying second hand. I don't know how long this opportunity will last.

By buying our clothes from charity shops, we will be able to replace our bad clothes with good ones. We'll be able to score an occasional bargain, or buy an occasional treat without parting with big money, we can build up a non-polluting wardrobe, *and* we'll be supporting good causes. I mean, why wouldn't you? This is a win/win for everybody.

It took me a while of snapping up bargains to build up a quality wardrobe that would last me a long time, but that wasn't a problem. Woe is me, I've got to go out and find myself better clothes? We wish we could have these problems. Now my wardrobe is fully natural, and I'm much better dressed than I would ever have been able to afford if I'd had to buy new.

"But what about all the clothes I already have?" you might be saying. "Most of my clothes contain artificial fabrics of some kind or other. What can I do to stop them from polluting the environment? Do I have to throw them away? Or stop wearing them? Isn't that kind of wasteful?"

That *is* kind of wasteful. And the garment that you have now is not going to stop shedding plastic microfibers if you give it away to the charity shop. It will simply be bought by somebody else.

There are no really good solutions to this problem, but there are some ways in which you can mitigate it.

1. As we've said before - buy no more plastic clothes. Then at least you have stopped your part of the problem increasing.
2. Sign this petition[72] to ask the government to phase out all non-essential plastics.
3. Do what you can to stop microfibers from washing out of your clothes and down the washing machine's outlet pipe to the sea.
4. Do what you can to stop microfibers from blowing out of your tumble-dryer and into the atmosphere.

We've got number 1 and 2. How do we do 3 and 4?

The easiest way of tackling number 4 is to stop using your tumble-dryer. The heavy wear on your garments caused by the tumble dryer—all that heat and knocking into things and being exposed to blasts of hot air—mean more microfibers are shed in the drying process than would be shed by gentle wear. Keep those garments out of the dryer and the environment will thank you, your clothes will last longer and your energy bill will go down.

But we can't stop washing our clothes, so what can we do to prevent microfibers from going with the water down the drain? How do we tackle number 3?

Firstly, as with the dryer, we're going to minimize how much the clothes are stressed by being flapped, wrung and knocked during the wash. This means:

● Fill the drum fuller—the less the clothes move around, the less their surfaces are abraded, and the fewer microfibers break off.

● Wash less frequently.

● Wash at a lower temperature.

---

72. https://friendsoftheearth.uk/plastics/microfibres-plastic-in-our-clothes

- Use a gentler spin speed.

Secondly, we can attempt to filter the fibers out of the water before it leaves the machine. There are several ways that I know of to do this.

You can use a Cora Ball[73]. The Cora ball is a laundry ball inspired by the shape of coral, which makes its living from sieving particles out of the ocean. You just pop the cora ball in your washing machine with the clothes, and it claims to remove up to 26% of microfibers before they leave the wash. 26% might not sound like much, but a 26% improvement is better than no improvement at all.

FOR A MUCH BETTER FILTRATION rate, you can use a GuppyFriend Washing Bag[74]. This is a smallish fabric bag with a coated inner side into which you place your artificial fiber clothes before you put the bag into the washing machine. The bag reduces friction to the clothes, causing fewer fibers to break off, and it prevents any fibers that do break off from leaving the bag, so that only clean water goes down the drain.

My children and I rather enjoyed using the 'bag of shame' as we christened it, and I've seen many positive reviews for it online. My own problem with it is that it keeps your clothes together in a single mass, and that leads to a very uneven pressure during the spin cycle. The whole machine is unbalanced and ends up shaking itself across the floor. A few months after we started using the Guppy bag, our washing machine died.

This may have been a coincidence of course. But it wasn't a coincidence I was willing to risk happening twice. Plastic waste is bad, but throwing away a whole washing machine every few months is untenable.

---

73.   https://coraball.com/

74. https://www.theplasticfreeshop.co.uk/guppy-friend-washing-bag

On reflection, what I should have done was to load the washing machine drum as full as possible, and then make a hollow in the center of the load and place the Guppy bag in there so that it couldn't move around. After losing one washing machine, however, I was not willing to risk it again.

OUR EVENTUAL SOLUTION was to buy a microfiber filter from Filtrol[75]. We installed this in the outflow pipe of the washing machine, and it now hangs on the wall beside the machine, filtering the water as it leaves. Every month or so we have to clean the filter out and dispose of the horrendously smelling gunk inside, but it's a small price to pay for not having to worry about the damage we're doing to the environment with every wash.

As I mentioned, it was How to Give Up Plastic: A Guide to Changing the World, One Plastic Bottle at a Time[76], by Will McCallum which started me on this part of my journey. At the time I was simply inspired to get rid of plastic in my life in order to do my part in saving the world, and I was encouraged that McCallum's book made that sound doable.

What I didn't expect was that in getting rid of plastic I would find that I much preferred the alternatives. I expected a journey of privation and sacrifice, but what I got was unexpected improvement across the board.

My clothes were now more comfortable, higher quality. I felt better dressed. I *smelled nicer* because my home-made deodorant and talc smelled of natural essential oils rather than having that weird back-of-the-throat chemical smell. My *house* smelled nicer because my cleaning products also smelled of natural oils rather than chemicals. Instead of being choked with a litter of plastic bottles, my bathroom

75. https://filtrol.net/

76.   https://www.amazon.co.uk/How-Give-Plastic-spokesperson-anti-plastic/dp/0241363217

shelf had glass and ceramic containers which I actually enjoyed looking at. When I went out, it was with a basket over my arm and a feeling of preparedness that only got better when I could bring out exactly what I needed to do my shopping with instead of helplessly accepting whatever plastic container I was being offered.

There is something very—I hate to use the word 'healing' because it sounds so New Agey, but—there is something very healing about being surrounded by natural products rather than artificial ones. You can feel, somehow, that those things are more—gah, there's that word again—wholesome, more healthy. Surrounding yourself with things that are not actively killing the planet feels good. It feels like something in you is giving a sigh of relief. I have received more in the process of going plastic free than I have ever had to give up.

So of course once I had mostly got on top of the plastic use, I started looking for other places where I could do better. What else could I do to save the world, and improve my own life in the process?

CHAPTER THREE
Greener Living

ONCE I HAD ORDERED my lifestyle to become as plastic-free as possible, I wanted to do more. After all, although it's a big problem, plastic is not the only source of our environmental woes.

It's surprising that we got through a full quarter of the book without mentioning climate change, but we've arrived there now.

According to the Met Office (that is, the UK's official meteorological office, which observes and predicts the weather and has been doing so since 1854,)

"the level of carbon dioxide in the atmosphere rose by 40% during the 20th and 21st century and is now over 400ppm (parts per million). This level of carbon dioxide is higher than at any time in the past 800,000 years...

"One-quarter of human-made greenhouse gas emissions come from burning fossil fuels for electricity and heat production.

"Another quarter of human-made greenhouse gas emissions comes from Agriculture, Forestry, and Other Land Use (AFOLU)....

"If we want to avoid significant increases in the average surface temperature, we must cut greenhouse gas emissions and switch to renewable energy sources. We must also use land more sustainably and may need to use techniques to remove carbon dioxide from the air.

If we continue to burn fossil fuels and cut down forests at the same rate, the planet could warm by more than 4°C by 2100. This warming could fundamentally change life on earth, with potentially drastic consequences."

- The Met Office[1]

By reducing consumption of plastic and therefore demand for plastic, we are beginning to do something to reduce part of the industry that consumes fossil fuels, and we are helping to reduce the kind of pollution that prevents the earth from healing itself. That's great. But there are a lot of other things we can do to help save the world.

According to the Met Office, one quarter of the greenhouse gas emissions we're pumping into the atmosphere comes from burning fossil fuels for electricity and heat.

Transport varies by country, but in the UK[2] burning petrol and diesel for transport in cars, trains and planes is responsible for 26% of the country's greenhouse gas emissions, and in the US[3] it's responsible for about a third of the country's output.

So what can we do to reduce greenhouse gas emissions from electricity use, heat production and transport?

Energy Use

THE FIRST AND EASIEST step we can take with our own personal energy use is to switch our energy provider from one which relies on fossil fuels to one which provides energy from renewable resources such as solar power, wind power, off-shore wave power etc.

In the UK there are several companies to choose from when it comes to 100% renewable electricity, but very few provide 100% renewable gas as well. Those which do not supply renewable gas do however make up for it by 'carbon-offsetting' their gas. Carbon offsetting means that they contribute to programs which should scrub an equivalent amount of carbon dioxide out of the air to that their gas releases into it, leaving them carbon neutral at the end of it.

Here is a list, current as of date of publication, of the UK's top green energy suppliers.[1]

I'm with Bulb, and very happy with them.

So that's sorted, right? I've done my bit for the environment as regards energy and I can move on to the next thing?

Well... yes and no.

---

1.   https://usave.co.uk/energy/green-energy-suppliers/

Even if all you do is to switch to a green energy supplier you have already done a great thing. You're part of the mass movement that is already beginning to pry the stranglehold of fossil fuels from around the world's neck, and you can be proud of yourself.

But there's always more that we can do. Globally, the demand for energy is going up and up as the inhabitants of more countries reach for a standard of living equivalent to what we have in the West.

"Per capita energy consumption today averages just 2.5 kW worldwide. Lifting all of humanity to the current US standard of living by 2100—an average of 9.5 kW per person, probably a conservative projection—thus means generating more than 51 TW of energy on top of everything we already produce today.

In our thought experiment, the year 2100 will thus see demand reach a mind-boggling 70 TW. Take every coal-fired generator, nuclear power plant, wind turbine, and solar farm and then multiply it by four." — Anthropocene Magazine[2]

Wind turbines and solar power arrays still require energy and materials to manufacture them. Batteries require rare earths and minerals that need to be mined from whichever parts of the world they can be found in. The silica and steel all have to come from somewhere, and our planet's supplies of such things are finite.

The last thing we want is for the rest of the world to have to suffer just so that we can carry on having our unfettered access to power, so as global population continues to rise, and energy demands continue to rise with it, we have to let go of the idea that energy is unlimited. In the First World, we use a year's worth of the Earth's resources every seven months.[3] We are essentially using our planet up and squeezing it dry by overspending our resources. Unfortunately, if everyone is to have a

2.   https://www.anthropocenemagazine.org/howmuchenergy/

3.   https://www.independent.co.uk/news/
        earth-overshoot-day-natural-resources-humans-planet-nature-damage-global-footprint-a846075
        6.html

decent standard of living, those of us in rich countries will have to start using less.

How do I reduce my energy footprint?

1. Heating

Turn the thermostat down in your house.

In the summer the house heating can simply be switched off.

In the winter, try to keep the temperature between 18-20 degrees C.

If you work at home and you're sitting for long periods of time, this will feel cold. Instead of whacking the heating back up, though, put on several layers of clothes, including thermals.

I write at home, and can get thoroughly chilled. So I bought myself some fake fur material and made myself a floor-length 'fur' coat to wear indoors. It's very stylish. I lined it with silk, and I wear it with sheepskin slippers and a sheepskin hat. I feel like a steppe nomad hardily doing my work while the winds of the tundra sweep across the permafrost. It's very romantic, and usually quite warm enough, although on especially cold days I will stuff a hot water bottle down it for that extra pot-bellied effect.

A duvet wrapped around yourself is just as effective if you would prefer not to go that far.

Other things you can do to avoid getting cold—

Insulate your house! Put in as much insulation as you can afford in the loft and in the walls. There are a wide variety of types of eco-friendly insulation[4], and you'll get the benefit of this in the summer too as your house will remain cooler in the increasingly hot summers.

Block out drafts. Welcome back the long lost presence of draft-excluders—either the utilitarian brushes that you can screw to the bottom of your doors, the kind that you make yourself[5] out of waste

---

4.   https://www.ecomerchant.co.uk/walls/insulation.html

5.   https://www.ovoenergy.com/blog/lifestyle/

make-your-own-sausage-dog-draft-excluder.html

material and stuff with all that bubble-wrap you don't know what to do with, or something a bit whackier like this unicorn draft excluder.[6]

Double glaze your windows, with glass if you can afford it, or with window insulating clingfilm[7] if you can't.

Get yourself heavy, thermally insulating curtains if you can afford it, or pin towels on the backs of the curtains you do have, if you can't.

Speaking of increasingly hot summers, I know the temptation is to buy yourself an air-conditioner for those weeks where the temperature goes over 30 degrees, but if that can possibly be resisted it should be. Those things are as thirsty for power as the tumble dryer.

In hot seasons the trick is also to insulate. Keep the heat out of the house for as long as you can.

In the cool of the early morning, late evening and night, open every window you can to allow the day's built up heat to dissipate. Be aware of the outside temperature, and when the outside temperature begins to edge higher than the inside temperature, close all those windows and draw your heavy insulating curtains over them. Shut the heat outside as you would with the winter cold.

After a run of hot days and hot nights the house will warm up anyway, and then you may have to resort to solutions such as keeping your hair damp, or even building yourself one of these home-made solar powered air conditioners.

In the long run, it may be worth your while to get solar panels attached to your house and run heating and/or cooling units from those. Even with government assistance for the purchase, this is a major decision, however, which not all of us are able to afford.

6.　https://www.ebay.co.uk/itm/

Soft-Plush-Unicorn-Draught-Draft-Excluder-Door-Window-Cushion-Energy-Saver-New/

382585001435?hash=item5913d7d5db:g:cCsAAOSwAclbu4~x

7.　https://www.ebay.co.uk/sch/

i.html?_from=R40&_trksid=p2047675.m570.l1313.TR2.TRC1.A0.H0.Xdouble+glazing+fil

m.TRS0&_nkw=double+glazing+film&_sacat=0

2. Reduce energy use via devices

• When you have to replace your household appliances try to get new energy efficient ones.

• The tumble-dryer is a massive energy-hog. Consider just not having one. In the summer, you can dry your clothes on a clothesline outside. For the winter, I absolutely recommend a ceiling clothes airer on a pulley[8]. Put this on the top floor of your house, to take advantage of the fact that hot air rises, and you will be able to dry a washing machine load of clothes approximately every three days. I've been using one of these for years, and unlike airers at floor level, I've never yet had a load stay damp long enough to get that musty 'hasn't dried fast enough' smell.

• Front loading washing machines are much more efficient than top-loading ones. If you can, get one with eco settings, and run it at the lowest temperature you can that still gets the dirt out. People have advised me to wash with cold water, but I suspect that they live in soft water areas, as my clothes come out just as dirty as they went in if the water is cold. I use a 30 degree wash, which is fine for everything (too high for wool. Wool does well when washed cold.)

Try to use your washing machine less often, so wear your clothes for longer. Pants and socks need to be fresh every day, but shirts can go two to three days before they need washing, and trousers can go a week.

When you do put the washing machine on, fill the drum full. Your mum as well as mine probably told you to leave a third of the drum empty to allow the clothes to move around freely. Which yes, probably

---

8. https://www.castinstyle.co.uk/section.php/2/1/traditional-pulley-clothes-airers

does create a superior clean, but it's not worth losing the planet over a few stubborn stains.

- Dishwasher or not? Most[9] of the sources[10] I read now claim that using a dishwasher is more eco-friendly than washing your dishes by hand, *provided* that you are using a modern, efficient machine. But you should only run it when it's full, and you should not use the rinse-hold, pre-rinse or heat-dry settings.

In the summer, when it's very hot and the water butts in the garden have been drained, I prefer to hand-wash so that I can take the waste water outside and use it to water my plants. This beats the water-use efficiency of even the most up to date device, but it's of less use in the winter when everything is already soaked. If you have a large garden, and you want to graduate to serious eco-warrior status, you can consider re-plumbing the outlets of your bath, shower, sinks, washing machine and dishwasher so that the used water (known as 'grey water') goes into irrigating the garden. But this is the advanced level, which I haven't reached yet, partly because my garden is too small to absorb that amount of water.

Speaking of water, though, water is also an energy use issue[11]. Treating water to bring it to the drinkable standard that flows through our taps takes energy. Pumping that treated water up hill and down dale to our taps takes energy. The water industry does not know whether the UK will be hotter and drier in 2050 than it is now, or hotter and wetter, but they do know that there will be more people and more demand for

---

9. https://www.greenchoices.org/green-living/at-home/
   is-it-greener-to-hand-wash-or-use-a-dishwasher

10. https://www.thoughtco.com/are-dishwashers-good-for-environment-1203932

11.   https://assets.publishing.service.gov.uk/government/uploads/system/uploads/
   attachment_data/file/291635/scho1209brob-e-e.pdf

water, and more demand for water equals more energy that has to come from somewhere.

Being more frugal with the amount of water we use is a virtue that may soon become a necessity. So we can help by getting a head start and deliberately reducing our water usage now.

How to reduce water usage.

I'm sure you've heard this all before, but we'll recap:

- Do not leave the water running when cleaning your teeth.

- If washing your dishes manually, use as few basin-fulls as possible, and ideally use the dirty water for something else (such as watering your plants) afterward.

- Put a brick or a waste plastic bottle filled with sand into the cistern of your toilet—this will mean it uses less water with each flush.

- Wash your hair less often—it really doesn't need it. Your hair will get used to whatever frequency you wash it at. If you start to wash it every day it will begin to need it every day. If, like me, you wash it once a week, it will only begin to get greasy toward the end of the week.

- Have a full-body wash less often. (Wash your groin and armpits using a sink full of water and a wash-cloth each day and save baths and showers as weekly luxuries.) The other parts of you simply do not get that dirty over the course of a week.

A bath filled about a third of the way up (which takes the water level over your belly button when you lie down) requires around 75 litres. An ordinary electrically heated shower puts out four litres per minute. So a 19-minute shower is just more than a bath. If you have a power shower, flow rates could be doubled and you'd need just 10 minutes. - Science Focus Magazine[12]

This means that if you spend half an hour in the shower every morning, you're actually using over five times more water than someone who has a bath once a week. Good news for those of us who enjoy a long soak in some eco-friendly bubbles.

Semi-Hardcore toilet options.

Having mentioned the brick-in-the-toilet-cistern trick, I also want to mention the hardcore option for those people who have gardens.

For optimum yield and health, gardens need fertilizer. It so happens that human urine is the perfect mix of nitrogen, potassium and other trace elements that the soil needs. You *could* flush away huge volumes of increasingly precious water so that the dilute urine will have to be dealt with at the sewage treatment works, and then buy chemical fertilizers for your garden which end up killing your soil. OR, you could not bother with the toilet at all - you could collect your urine in a bucket or chamber pot and throw it on your garden.

I've seen advice out there that suggests you should dilute the urine and you shouldn't allow it to touch the foliage or it might scorch it, but I figured that animals do not dilute their urine when they pee on the ground, and if grass could thrive on the output of a herd of cows or sheep, it could survive mine. And I was right. You should see how lovely and green my lawn is now.

These days I use the bucket which lives in my downstairs loo for all visits that are purely liquid. I wipe with cloth which I wash at the same time as I wash my hands. The urine goes on the lawn and the bucket gets rinsed out from the garden water butt and replaced for next time.

This way, I only have to use the toilet—and the toilet paper—once a day. It's a massive saving on water *and* paper.

---

12.   https://www.sciencefocus.com/science/
how-long-does-a-shower-have-to-be-to-use-the-same-amount-of-water-as-a-bath/

If you do not have a garden, you can save flush water by only flushing liquids once a day. There's a saying I overheard recently that goes "If it's brown, flush it down. If it's yellow, let it mellow."

I tried this, but in practice letting a toilet full of pee sit there all day leads to your toilet very rapidly acquiring unsightly stains. You then have to clean it more often, which results in pouring more chemicals into the water processing system.

I propose, as a refinement on this scheme, that you use a covered bucket to pee into, and pour the contents down the toilet only when the bucket is full. That way you can minimize water use and keep your porcelain clean at the same time.

The hardest core toilet option, of course, is to use a composting toilet for liquids *and* solids. I have not looked into this one because I'm looking for quick and easy things for regular people to do, and I suspect that installing composting toilets is a little extreme for most of us.

Transport

THERE ISN'T REALLY enough to say here to justify a whole chapter to itself, but it means I get to add another little picture, so here we are.

What is there to say about transport that you don't know? Transport creates 28% of the total output of the world's greenhouse gasses (GHGs.) That's more even than the energy business (which comes in at 27%.)

GHG gasses are emitted in the fuel refining stage as well as when aviation fuel, petrol or diesel is burned to move a vehicle around. And unlike the energy sector—in which there has been a big increase in the use of renewable fuels—transportation has not shown a similar shift to environmentally friendly options. That may begin to change now adverts for electric and hybrid cars are all over the TV though. We can hope.

Long distance travel

In terms of greenhouse gas emissions, the very worst thing you can do for the planet is to take a plane for a short haul journey, for example by flying from London to Glasgow. Most of the fuel is expended on take-off and landing, so by taking off and landing in a short distance you are expending more fuel per journey than someone who was flying a long way.

Taking a plane for a long haul flight comes in at the second worst travel option for the environment.

This means that if you really want to be an eco-warrior, you may have to reconsider your holidays. Do you have to fly to Ibiza this summer? Do you have to jet off for a skiing trip in January? Could you, perhaps, go by train, or by boat? Or not go at all?

If you cannot put off a plane trip, the way to reduce your emissions is to make sure that the plane is as full as it can be—so the emissions are spread out over a larger number of people traveling. Try to go during peak times, when there will be no spare seats. Choose economy class, because business and first class involve more empty space and therefore lower efficiency. And choose direct routes without stop-overs, to minimize the number of times the plane has to take-off and land.

After the plane, the next worst method of travel is the diesel or petrol car, if driven by a single person and otherwise empty.

Per km traveled, the car produces 171g of emissions, while a long-haul plane flight produces 195g. As you can see, there's really not a lot in it! I don't know about you, but I had not fully realized until now that driving the (petrol) car on my own was almost as bad as taking a plane.

Taking the bus (104g) is better than driving if you are driving only yourself. But if you take three other people in your car, then the car is better than the bus (43g.)

Taking a train is better still, and a long-distance coach is even better than that, with Eurostar being best of all for long-distance travel at 6g per km.

Every-day travel

But if you're anything like me, the majority of your travel will not be long-distance to foreign countries. It will be to and from work and to the shops for groceries.

Here, unless you fly to work, the worst culprit by far is the single person in a fossil-fuel powered car. If you drive your empty car to work and back then you will be releasing 170g of greenhouse gasses every kilometer. Anything else would be better.

Alternatives to (petrol/diesel) car travel - low commitment

Can you take the train to work? Can you take the bus? Can you pick up three colleagues and share the journey?

Alternatives to (petrol/diesel) car travel - high commitment

If you work more than 10 miles away from where you live, can you trade in your (petrol/diesel) car for an electric car?

The electric car in itself creates 0g in greenhouse gas emissions when it's being used. If you charge it up from a source of renewable energy, such as your own charging point at home—where you're with a company that supplies renewable energy—then it creates 0g in greenhouse gas emissions while it's being charged too.

This report from Carbon Brief website[13] addresses the carbon costs of manufacturing the electric car, and of charging it when you're not clear where the energy is coming from:

- *EVs are responsible for considerably lower emissions over their lifetime than conventional (internal combustion engine) vehicles across Europe as a whole.*

- *In countries with coal-intensive electricity generation, the benefits of EVs are smaller and they can have similar lifetime emissions to the most efficient conventional vehicles – such as hybrid-electric models.*

- *However, as countries decarbonise electricity generation to meet their climate targets, driving emissions will fall for existing EVs and manufacturing emissions will fall for new EVs.*

- *In the UK in 2019, the lifetime emissions per kilometre of driving a Nissan Leaf EV were about three times lower than*

13.   https://www.carbonbrief.org/
factcheck-how-electric-vehicles-help-to-tackle-climate-change

*for the average conventional car, even before accounting for the
falling carbon intensity of electricity generation during the car's
lifetime.*

If you work less than ten miles away from where you live, can you
trade in your (petrol/diesel) car for an electric bike?

An article by Forbes[14] says:

*"In the best of cases, E-bikes are charged using low-carbon energy
sources like residential solar panels, but even if powered by a dirtier
electricity grid, they are still the most energy-efficient form of motorized
transport, consuming the electricity equivalent of about 1,000 miles per
gallon of gasoline[15]. A study[16] by the Institute for Transportation and
Development Policy shows that transportation mode-shifting to bicycles
and E-bikes—increasing from about 7% today to approximately 22%
of urban passenger travel distance worldwide by 2050—would reduce
emissions 47% and save $128 trillion compared to business-as-usual."*

I am a huge fan of the electric bike, having replaced my car with
one in June 2019. I call him Vinnie, and he's a Gazelle Vento C7, a
splendid—if rather somberly colored machine.

I live 7.5 miles from our local town and cycle there three times a
week to buy my groceries. (I work at home.)

Instead of being one more empty car contributing to the traffic
jams on the road, and belching out almost as many GHGs as an
airplane, I zip down the cycle path. Sometimes I pedal smugly past the
cars as they sit in a tailback that stretches for miles.

---

14.   https://www.forbes.com/sites/energyinnovation/2017/07/06/
         as-transportation-costs-emissions-grow-electric-bikes-offer-an-efficient-alternative/#a5c02393e5
         9c943d6a75a9241140faca34e029cb3305a

15.   *https://www.forbes.com/sites/wadeshepard/2016/05/18/*
         as-china-chokes-on-smog-the-biggest-adoption-of-green-transportation-in-history-is-being-banned/
         2/#a5c02393e59c943d6a75a9241140faca33fe318952662

16.   *https://www.itdp.org/a-global-high-shift-cycling-scenario/*

I put my shopping in my saddlebags, and if it's heavy I switch the assist mode up one level and let the bike add extra power to my legs. It's a great feeling to be able to make the bike fly even when I'm feeling weak. Hills and headwinds don't trouble me at all.

When I bought the bike I had been told by my physiotherapist that I had to strengthen my thigh muscles or I would soon be unable to stand up. I was already dependent on a cane to hobble around. But now I'm cycling three times a week I can also walk without difficulty, and I'm fitter now than I ever have been.

I charge the battery about once a fortnight. But that is because Lithium batteries are happiest if they are not allowed to run down. I've never got below three out of five bars of charge, and the household electricity bills did not even register a noticeable uptick when the e-bike joined us. As you can imagine, the saving on petrol money alone is considerable, even without factoring in the benefits to the environment and my health.

Working from home

In these Covid-influenced days, I no longer need to argue how much better it would be if those of us who could work from home did so. We've all now discovered that meetings can be held over Zoom or Discord, home computers can be linked to work servers, and there is very little need for us to all be in the same building for eight hours a day.

Continuing to work at home will mean that expensive office buildings do not have to be heated in the winter or air-conditioned in the summer. Petrol and diesel will not need to be burned to transport us to these unnecessary places and back. In the best of all worlds, the offices could be abandoned, and the land given over to housing the homeless, or sustainable agriculture, or simply re-wilded and allowed to go back to nature. Imagine the food forests we could grow in their places!

Clothes

WE TALKED ABOUT CLOTHES made from artificial fibers back in the 'Bedroom' chapter, and recommended buying only natural fiber clothes in future. And we talked about issues with microfibers, and how to minimize energy use on washing and drying clothes in the laundry and energy use chapters. So what is there left to say about clothes?

Quite a lot, actually.

Surprisingly, the fashion industry "accounts for 10 percent of global carbon emissions and remains the second largest industrial polluter, second only to oil. Fast fashion items are often worn less than 5 times, kept for roughly 35 days, and produce over 400 percent more carbon emissions per item per year than garments worn 50 times and kept for a full year." - Green Matters[17]

'Fast fashion' is the sort of thing sold at Primark. Clothes that are so very up to the moment that in a month they'll be behind the times. Clothes that are so cheap, you decide to buy three of them even though you aren't sure when you'll ever wear them.

"Fast fashion focuses on speed and low costs in order to deliver frequent new collections inspired by catwalk looks or celebrity styles.

---

17.   https://www.greenmatters.com/style/2018/08/28/ybXGX/
        fast-fashion-impacts-environment

But it is particularly bad for the environment, as pressure to reduce cost and the time it takes to get a product from design to shop floor means that environmental corners are more likely to be cut. Criticisms of fast fashion include its negative environmental impact, water pollution, the use of toxic chemicals and increasing levels of textile waste." - The Independant[18]

Cutting costs of manufacture often leads to garment producers setting up their factories in poverty stricken countries where they can pay slave-wages for child labor.

"Child labour can be found at all levels of the fashion industry, and nowhere is this more evident than with the production of cotton. In the cotton industry, children are often used[19] to cross-pollinate the cotton plants, to harvest the crop, and in spinning, weaving and dyeing mills." - Good on You[20]

Textiles make up around 3% of the average household bin in the UK. In West London alone it's estimated that almost 9,000 tonnes of textiles end up in our bins or bags. If we reuse or recycle these items instead we could save a whopping 39 million tonnes of carbon!" - GetSwishing.com[21]

A lot of the problem stems from the fact that the clothing industry is a global industry. Firms in London buy cotton from Uzbekistan and have it woven and dyed - using cheap, toxic dyes - in Bangladesh, only to sell it in Australia for less money than it would cost even to buy the raw materials in the UK.

The cotton is grown using pesticides that kill the soil and run off into the waters to create dead zones in the ocean. And to irrigate this mass produced cotton the country's aquifers are drained—1.5 trillion

---

18.   https://www.independent.co.uk/life-style/fashion/
        environment-costs-fast-fashion-pollution-waste-sustainability-a8139386.html

19.   https://www.bbc.com/news/world-asia-16639391

20.   https://goodonyou.eco/child-labour/

21.   http://getswishing.com/

liters of water are used a year in the fashion industry, often in countries that are otherwise struggling to provide their people with drinking water.

So not even cotton is safe!

What can we do to find clothes that are not going to destroy the environment and exploit children?

First of all, let's be sure to boycott the firms who are known to be destroying the environment and exploiting children. I'm afraid this involves a bit of research into your favourite clothing brand's ethical trading and ecological footprints. Happily a lot of the high street shops are aware that customers are becoming more demanding when it comes to eco-credentials, and they are beginning to promise to clean up their acts. Whether they will actually follow through remains to be seen, and it's important to keep pressure on them until they do.

Rather than buy from the high street before they've reformed their practices, buying second hand from charity shops or ebay is worth recommending again.

There are also local groups helping to organize clothing swaps. Perhaps you really want a change, but your clothes are perfectly good? It makes sense to get in touch with a lot of other people in the same situation and swap things around until you have a completely new (to you) wardrobe for nothing, and with no use of extra resources at all.

You can find clothing swap groups on Meetup.com[22], GetSwishing.com[23], Gumtree,[24] Eventbrite,[25] local swap shops,[26] or if there are none near you, you can always host a swapping event yourself.

If you need something in a hurry and can't swap for it, you can't go wrong with the following principles:

---

22.   https://www.meetup.com/topics/clothesswap/

23.   http://getswishing.com/

24.   https://www.gumtree.com/swap-shop

25.   https://www.eventbrite.co.uk/d/united-kingdom--london/clothes-swap/

26.   https://www.timeout.com/london/shopping/best-swap-shops-in-london

Buy natural fibers.

Check out the track record of the shop and buy from a retailer which scores well for ethical practices on Ethical Consumer.[27]

Buy items you think you will enjoy wearing for many years, and which are well-made enough that they should last for many years. We're no longer following fashion, we're dressing to save the world.

Ideally buy from a retailer using locally, sustainably/organically grown material, manufactured in local factories, dyed with natural dyes and sewn by a local labour force.

Super-ideally, buy from a Fibershed[28] producer.

"Fibershed develops regional and regenerative fiber systems on behalf of independent working producers, by expanding opportunities to implement carbon farming, forming catalytic foundations to rebuild regional manufacturing, and through connecting end-users to farms and ranches through public education.

We envision the emergence of an international system of regional textile communities that enliven connection and ownership of 'soil-to-soil' textile processes. These diverse textile cultures are designed to build soil carbon stocks on the working landscapes on which they depend, while directly enhancing the strength of regional economies. Both fiber and food systems now face a drastically changing climate, and must utilize the best of time-honored knowledge and available science for their long-term ability to thrive." - Fibershed[29]

I'm very excited about Fibershed, which does for clothing what restoration agriculture does for food—it aims to grow the plants and/or animals from which clothing fibers are sourced in such a way as to actually repair the soil. This is not merely 'sustainable' fashion which aims to not make the situation worse—this is fashion that aims to draw

---

27.   https://www.ethicalconsumer.org/fashion-clothing/shopping-guide/
          high-street-clothes-shops

28.   https://fibershed.org/

29.   https://fibershed.org/about/

down carbon from the atmosphere and reverse global warming at the same time as it gives local people a chance to earn a living, and gives buyers a chance to have a garment that is precious because it's hand crafted and doing good in the world.

It's only a nascent movement in the world, with only a couple of chapters in the UK, but it's something I'll jump at the chance of supporting as it grows.

Food

HAVING TOUCHED ON HOW the fibers for our clothes are grown, we're beginning to get back to the most basic necessities of life, so let's carry on that trend by thinking about food.

On first thoughts you probably would not imagine that agriculture was a major source of damage to the environment. We're used to thinking of farming as a bucolic life, nurturing the land and reaping its bounty. The trouble is that since the 'green revolution' on the invention of fertilizers, pesticides and industrial agriculture, there has been a lot more reaping than there has been nurturing.

Modern industrial agriculture is, in fact, one of the major drivers of climate change, contributing 14 per cent of total greenhouse gas emissions—and that's without the deforestation and pollution for which it's also responsible.

Fossil fuels are used throughout modern agriculture. Fossil fuels go into the chemical factories that brew fertilizer and herbicides. Fossil fuels are burned by farming machinery like tractors and harvesters. Fossil fuels are burned by the fleets of vehicles—including aircraft—needed to ship agricultural produce all over the world. If you're sitting down to a meal of Brazilian grown beef cooked in olive oil from Greece, with sweetcorn from the US and sweet potato from South Africa, you can imagine how much the air miles and jet fuel pile up.

But it's worse than that.

Even apart from the use of fossil fuels in agriculture, turning over the soil exposes the carbon stored in the soil to the sun's UV light. Every time a field is ploughed, carbon is exposed to the air, where it combines with oxygen and is emitted in the form of carbon dioxide.

"Dr. Rattan Lal, Professor of Soil Science at Ohio State University, has calculated that over the last 150 years, 476 billions of tonnes of carbon has been emitted from farmland soils due to inappropriate farming and grazing practices, compared with 'only' 270 Gt emitted from of burning of fossil fuels."

- World Future Council[30]

Sadly, it's even worse than that. All over the world—and famously in the Amazon rainforest—valuable ecosystems that have been functioning as the lungs of the earth, drawing down carbon dioxide and putting out oxygen, are being cut down to make room for more soy, corn and cattle.

Overuse of herbicides and pesticides are killing off the friendly biological processes in the soil that enhance soil fertility, leading to farmers becoming dependent on chemical fertilizers. But chemical fertilizers are washing out of the soil, entering the water table, and causing algal blooms in the oceans which pump the oceans full of toxins[31] and create huge dead zones.

As if to add insult to injury, the cows for whom this ecological vandalism is being committed are a large source of methane emissions, and methane is a worse GHG than CO2.

To put it simply, the way we produce our food is a major factor in how we're killing our planet.

So what should we do? Should we go vegan? Will that solve everything?

---

30.   *https://www.worldfuturecouncil.org/how-does-agriculture-contribute-to-climate-change/*

31.   https://www.theguardian.com/environment/2020/jan/04/
          lethal-algae-blooms-an-ecosystem-out-of-balance

I've noticed that quite suddenly veganism is the in thing—you can now get vegan cakes at the coffee-shop, and there is usually a vegan alternative if you eat out. Many people are convinced that veganism is the way to save the world, and even government guidelines suggest that we should eat less meat in future, but I think it's a little more nuanced than "Vegetables are OK, meat is murder."

As you can see from what I've said already in this chapter, vegetables are murder too. The rainforest is not only being cut down for cattle. It's being cut down for soybeans and almond milk too. Indeed almond milk is one of the worst culprits in over-use of water, and has been linked to honey-bee colony collapse disorder[32].

Nutritionists have warned us that with a diet of mostly processed foods, a diet based on corn and corn syrup, malnutrition is on the rise even in wealthy areas of the world. But we can't solve that by importing Quinoa at a price that means now the locals can't afford it themselves, and forgetting how much jet fuel we're using to transport it.

The way we produce our vegetables, our rice, the wheat for our bread and pasta, the corn that we feed to our animals and which we turn into bio-diesel is a massive part of the problem. Giving up meat would not solve that.

Going vegan, in other words, isn't the solution we're looking for.

That's kind of terrifying, isn't it? We can't make a quick fix by simply cutting out one or two food items and doing more of everything else, because *everything* in the food system is broken. *Everything* is the problem.

So what can we do?

Let's start by cutting out as much of the fossil fuel use in our food as possible.

---

32.   https://www.theguardian.com/environment/2020/jan/07/
honeybees-deaths-almonds-hives-aoe

● **If possible, grow some of your own food.** - You can grow your salad plants on a windowledge, ensuring that not only are they as fresh as possible, but also that they don't come wrapped in plastic which you will have to throw away.

If you have outside space, consider turning it into a place where you can grow food. Even if it's a balcony, you can grow plants in containers, around the three outer walls, vertically up the inner wall and over the outside.

If you have a garden, you might even be able to grow all the veg you need right there using no-dig market-gardening techniques. Or you could turn it into a food forest by planting perennial edible plants—like fruit and nut trees—that just get bigger and more productive every year. More about this in the next chapter.

● *Shop from local farms.* - Reducing the miles your food has had to travel to get to you reduces the amount of fuel burned to transport it. It also means your food is a lot fresher than it would be if it had travelled around the world. So you get more vitamins.

● **Shop locally produced organically grown produce.** - Organically grown vegetables and grains do not use fossil-fuel based fertilizer, and have strict restrictions on herbicide and pesticide use. This not only reduces the amount of fossil fuels used and poisonous chemicals pumped into the environment, but damages the soil less and therefore helps retain carbon in the soil.

● **Buy locally produced organic/pasture-fed, free-range meat/dairy.** - Vegans are not wrong to draw attention to the appalling way animals are treated in our current system of meat production. In addition to being horribly cruel, industrial meat production leads to animals being pumped full of antibiotics—because they're being raised in conditions that make them sick—which leads to over use of antibiotics which end up in human food.

However, cows and sheep can be raised on land that is not suitable for crops. There is a lot of land where you can't get a tractor but you can let sheep graze, leading the sheep equivalent of a good life while producing sheep's milk, cheese, wool and eventually meat and sheepskin. Likewise, there's a lot of land in the world where the soil is too poor for agriculture, but cows can graze there, producing milk, yoghurt, cheese and eventually meat and leather.

Cows that are raised on pasture lead a natural, cruelty free life, *and* produce much less methane than those which are intensively fattened on grain. Their digestive systems simply didn't evolve to process grain, which left to their own devices they would not naturally eat. So again, the methane problem is a symptom of how broken our intensive agriculture system is, rather than a problem with cows themselves.

Eating locally produced, organic, pasture-raised meat is unfortunately expensive, which will in itself lead to a reduction in the amount of meat-eating. It will also protect the rainforest as well as any vegetarian could.

So. This whole half of the book has been about things you can reduce, recycle, give up and deny yourself. While worthy and necessary, that's a little depressing isn't it? Are you asking yourself, "Will this be enough? If I'm making all these sacrifices, will they work? IS THERE REALLY ANY HOPE?"

Having finished this section with food, I want to start the next section with food, because yes. There is hope. We are not helpless on this train to destruction. There is something we can do that will not only stop global warming but which has the potential to actually reverse it.

We can draw down carbon from the atmosphere. We can cool the planet. And what's more, we know how to do it, starting right now. And just as it was a big part of the problem, a big part of the solution is food.

Next chapter, hope.

CHAPTER FOUR
Solutions in the soil

"REGENERATIVE AGRICULTURE is a system of farming principles and practices that increases biodiversity, enriches soils, improves watersheds, and enhances ecosystem services.

Regenerative Agriculture aims to capture carbon in soil and aboveground biomass, reversing current global trends of atmospheric accumulation.

At the same time, it offers increased yields, resilience to climate instability, and higher health and vitality for farming and ranching communities.

The system draws from decades of scientific and applied research by the global communities of organic farming, agro-ecology, Holistic Management, and agro-forestry." - Regenerative Agriculture[1]

I'VE ALWAYS BEEN A science fiction fan, so when I pictured solutions to our global problems, I always thought they would be complicated and high-tech. I thought we would need to invent new devices and processes. Perhaps fusion power would save us? Or perhaps we could manufacture thousands of machines that sucked carbon out of the air and stored it somewhere safe?

It amuses me to think I was looking in quite the wrong direction. If I wanted a machine that sucked carbon out of the air and deposited it in the ground to enrich the soil, I should have realized that nature had already provided an infinite variety of them in the form of plants.

No machine for drawing carbon down from the atmosphere would do better than a tree, for example. And a tree is also providing shelter and food to hundreds of other species—insects, birds, microorganisms, squirrels, bats and so on. Not only that, the very same tree may be providing nuts or fruit for humans to eat, shading our increasingly hot cities and transpiring water from its leaves at the same time, helping to regulate the water-cycle.

Trees are of course not the only plants that draw carbon out of the atmosphere—all plants do it, in the process of photosynthesis. Marsh-lands and grass-lands like the African savanna do it too. In fact marshes and savanna are probably more resilient forms of carbon storage, since they are more resistant to prolonged drought and wildfires than forest.

If we want to reduce the amount of carbon dioxide in the air an easy and pleasant solution is simply to increase the amount of land given over to plants in the world.

---

1.   http://www.regenerativeagriculturedefinition.com/

But—and this is a big but—it's important to pay attention to the way those plants are grown.

I've told you about how agriculture contributes to global warming, haven't I? More intensively grown plants, fed with artificial fertilizer and cultivated by machines using fossil fuels will not do us any good. We need to learn—or perhaps re-learn—how to look after the world's natural systems so that they can look after us.

Let me tell you about how the soil, the plants and the very worms underfoot will save us, if we just stop killing them, and nurture them instead.

Regenerative agriculture and rewilding

The greatest carbon sink in the world is right under our feet—the soil. Billions of organisms are at work down there. No, that's an underestimation, because if you took a tablespoon of soil there would be billions of organisms in just that tiny amount. The majority of them are bacteria, and the majority of those are good, healthy bacteria, similar to the lactobacillus that we use to turn milk into yoghurt, regulate our gut health and ferment bread and beer.

These soil bacteria perform lots of useful functions: decomposing organic matter, promoting plant growth, improving the structure of the soil, making nutrients available to the roots of plants, drawing down nitrogen from the air and fixing it in the soil as a natural form of fertilizer and helping plants to resist infection.

In addition to bacteria, the soil is full of mycorrhizal fungi, which help plants to absorb other useful minerals such as phosphorus and zinc, and enable a kind of soil-wide-web of chemical information exchange and mutual aid. All of this, when it's healthy and active, eliminates the need for artificial fertilizer and helps plants to resist pests and remain healthy without the need for pesticides.

Worms carry the good bacteria in their guts, and as they travel through the soil they increase and spread the good ones, eat and reduce the bad ones. They also clean the soil of any heavy metal spills that might have come from human industry.

Plants, meanwhile, are splitting carbon dioxide up using photosynthesis to create oxygen and to make sugars out of the carbon. They feed the sugars out through their roots to help feed this mass of soil life in a friendly symbiosis with the organisms which are doing them so much good.

The end result is that plants are reducing carbon dioxide in the air where it is a harmful greenhouse gas, and converting it to carbon in the soil where it enriches the soil and makes it more fertile.

That's a win/win/win/win for us. We get oxygen, we get plants to eat, we get fertile soil *and* we get rid of carbon-dioxide from the atmosphere.

But this only works if we don't poison the soil organisms with artificial fertilizer, herbicides and pesticides, and we stop other practices that kill off the soil life too.

I think I've mentioned before that one of the big practices that kills off the beneficial organisms is ploughing the fields to grow the world's food crops. This slices up worms and exposes the good bacteria to the sun's UV rays, causing them to die off. The end result is that the soil is made less fertile and then the farmer has to start adding extra artificial fertilizer. The artificial fertilizer kills the soil off even more, and next year more fertilizer is needed. The end result is dirt that cannot support life, and desertification.

Interestingly, ploughing leading to desertification is not a new problem, though it has intensified greatly with the advent of modern farming. In Biblical times Lebanon was known for its cedar trees. Now it's mostly desert. In less ancient days, the US prairies were known for the staggering number of buffalo and other animals they supported. Now they too are rapidly turning to dust.

But we have to eat, and that means we have to grow food. Is there a way of doing it without destroying the planet?

Fortunately yes, the method is called Restorative Agriculture, and it's a big part of the solution.

Restorative/Restoration Agriculture

"The goal of a restoration agriculture system is to take advantage of all the benefits of natural, perennial ecosystems by creating agricultural systems that imitate nature in form and function while still providing for our food, building, fuel and other needs." - Mark Shepard

In the 1970s two men called Bill Mollison and David Holmgren looked at the way we grew our food and wondered why, when nature wants to grow perennial, long lasting plants, our food system relied on annual plants, which have to be replanted every year. What would happen if we grew food the way nature *wants* to grow plants?

From that question came the idea of *permaculture*. Permaculture is a portmanteau word made up of 'permanent' and 'agriculture' and the idea was to design a kind of agriculture that mimicked natural ecosystems and helped the earth to do what it does best—grow more and more fertile every year.

Permaculture started off in people's gardens, as people used the principles of looking after the soil, digging as little as possible, and designing the plants used to mimic nature to create gardens which provided them with fruit and vegetables and grew more productive each year as the perennial plants grew larger.

This was a great thing for anyone who had a garden—suddenly almost anyone could think about growing their own vegetables while improving the soil on their own patch. But it wasn't tackling the problem of large scale food production.

Then a number of farmers across the world began to work out how they could apply the permaculture principles of earth-care and ecosystem design to growing food in industrial quantities. Building on discoveries from a number of these, Mark Shepard[2] turned his normal, industrial farm first into alley-cropping system, and then into a sustainable food forest.

In a healthy forest there are tall trees, shorter trees that live in their shade, shrubs that live beneath those, ground cover plants, and a root layer, plus climbers that wind up all the layers.

Unable to make a living with his annual soy-bean and corn farm, Mark looked at which trees wanted to grow in his biome, and planted ones which produce valuable crops. For his tall trees he chose oaks for acorn flour and timber, sweet chestnuts for nuts and chestnut flour and pines for pine-nuts and wood. For the shorter trees he grew hazelnuts, all kinds of fruit trees, beeches and maples for sweet sap. Beneath

---

2.   https://youtu.be/5xKb8rPb2ps

that, the shrub layer contained all different kinds of berry bushes, and the plant layer beneath that could contain things like perennial kale, perennial broccoli, chard, spinach etc.

Through this forest of food, he would graze cows, sheep, pigs, hens, geese and guinea fowl, each animal feeding on its own preferred food—which was often the waste products of the farm, and the pests that would have otherwise damaged the plants.

As they were grazing, the animals deposited fertilizer in the form of manure and urine, meaning that no artificial fertilizers were needed.

Because none of the crops needed to be ploughed and resown every year, the soil could be left un-turned. The leaf-fall in the autumn was allowed to rot into it as another natural source of fertility. And Mark applied additional home-made compost every year, and sowed the ground with 'green manure'—plants that capture nitrogen from the atmosphere and fix it in the soil.

The end result was that his soil grew deeper and richer every year and the whole system became more and more productive without any input from fossil fuels at all.

The focus on tending to the soil resulted in both increased crop yield and—crucially—increased carbon in the soil.

Increased carbon in the soil meant that this farm was growing food while sucking carbon-dioxide out of the atmosphere.

In other words, this was a method of feeding ourselves *while reversing global warming.*

Mob Grazing

The good news doesn't stop there, because around the other side of the world in South Africa a man called Alan Savory[3] was investigating the growing deserts and degraded lands of Africa and trying to work out how to turn them back into lush savanna.

To cut a long story short, (I encourage you to look up his work on your own,) he found out that the natural behaviour of herds of

---

3.   https://www.youtube.com/watch?v=vpTHi7O66pI

herbivores is to graze in very large numbers on a piece of land for a short time before moving on before the lions or wolves can catch them.

If ranchers mimic this natural behaviour by bunching up their herds and keeping them moving, they can graze huge numbers of animals while actually improving the land and turning it back from desert into healthy grassland. And healthy grassland—you've guessed it—also sucks carbon-dioxide out of the atmosphere.

By harnessing the fertilizing powers of undisturbed soil and grazing animals we can reverse global warming, and reverse global desertification. We can turn the earth into a green and pleasant land again. And the constant refrain I've heard from those who've tried it is how surprised they are at how fast it can happen.

Rewilding

At about the same time that all of this was going on, a couple in the UK called Isabella Tree[4] and Charlie Burrell discovered that they were losing money hand over fist trying to farm their large estate at Knepp. They decided to turn their land back over to nature and began bringing in the kind of large animals that would have been present in the country before humans began to make them extinct.

They brought in deer, long-horn cattle, Exmoor ponies and Tamworth pigs in place of wild boar and allowed them to roam free and shape the landscape the way they would have done had they been wild.

Almost immediately, the ecosystem began to recover. Birds and insects that hadn't been seen for years began to reappear. And again, crucially, the soil began to recover from years of farming, and the estate turned into a carbon sink, helping to draw down carbon-dioxide from the atmosphere.

In the process they discovered that improving the soil improved water quality and water management.

---

4.   https://youtu.be/kvD1DGSS8Aw

Meanwhile in other rewilding projects elsewhere, the re-introduction of beavers into the landscape was discovered to prevent both floods and droughts, and the re-introduction of large predators caused a cascade of positive changes leading to recovery of biodiversity and soil health.

Essentially, the world knew what it was doing before we humans turned up and started to 'improve' things. If we just put things back as we found them—if we work with nature rather than against it—it will provide us with plentiful food, both meat and vegetables, and it will clean the air and solve our problems for us. Good news indeed!

This was a very compressed account of the good news that is permaculture/restoration agriculture/re-wilding, and I encourage you to look up some of the excellent books on the subject. I recommend "The Soil Will Save Us," by Kristin Ohlson[5] for a good place to start.

I don't want to re-hash something that other people have already done better and try to explain it all here. Instead, I want to move on to what this book is about—what we can do at home to help.

---

5.   http://www.kristinohlson.com/books/soil-will-save-us

How can we help?

IT'S GREAT TO HAVE good news, but unless you are a farmer—or otherwise have access to vast tracts of land—it can be hard to see how we can help with the long term project of enriching the soil. But we can, in our small way.

Gardening Basics

First of all, do you have a garden? If so, you too are a custodian over at least some of the world's soil. You can treat your garden in such a way that it becomes a fertile, lush oasis of land that is actively sucking carbon-dioxide out of the air.

How do I do that?

Learning to take care of your garden in an eco-friendly way requires un-learning some of the things you may currently do. An exhaustive list of best practices in the garden would require several books. So this one cannot cover it. You can learn all you need to know about permaculture from this free online, year-long permaculture course[6]. But I'll give you some basics to start off with so you can get started straight away.

Things to stop doing.

- Stop using artificial fertilizer. (Natural fertilizers like chicken manure or blood, fish and bone are fine.)

---

6.   https://www.freepermaculture.com/onlinecourse/

- Stop using weed-killer. Your weeds are valuable wild flowers, which can be considered as nature's white blood cells. If your soil has a deficiency, you can be sure a weed will turn up which will, over time, rectify that deficiency. Weeds are native wildflowers, and support a great biodiversity of insects and the birds, bats, frogs and toads that feed on them.

- Stop using pesticides. Using pesticides kills off not only the pests but all other beneficial insects with them, including vital pollinators and predatory insects which might otherwise have kept your pest insects in control. If you leave the insects alone, they will eventually establish a balance in which the beneficial insects keep the bad ones in check.

Artificial fertilizer, weed-killers and pesticides destroy the life in your soil and lead it to become less fertile over time. They also get on you and potentially cause asthma, immune system disorders and even cancer. There are organic alternatives to most pesticides—I've had a lot of success with just spraying the bugs with soapy water. We're going to get fertility into the soil in a more natural way, and as I mentioned, weeds are not a bad thing.

Things to start doing

- Cover your soil and keep it covered.

Just as soil that has been ploughed and is now exposed to the sun is soil where the life is dying off, so *any* soil which is exposed to the sun is soil in which the soil life is being irradiated to death by the sun's UV rays.

My parents had a rose garden which was essentially bare soil from which many spindly sticks of rose plants stood up. They spent a lot of time pulling up weeds from that soil, and even then I really never understood why a brown expanse of bare soil was considered a good thing. Now the verdict's in, and I was right. They should have grown other plants around the roses until no part of the soil remained bare.

Not only does this shield the soil life from the sun, but it shades the soil's surface and means that it retains water better, so you don't have to waste the water that is increasingly becoming a rare resource.

- Add more plants.

The more plants you have in a given area of soil, the more biodiversity there is, not only of the plants themselves, but also of the under-soil community. Lots of different worms, fungi and nematodes thrive when there are lots of different plants. Lots of different roots take up different nutrients from the soil and exude different compounds and minerals. Therefore, the more plants you have covering the soil, the richer that soil will become.

Perhaps you don't know what to plant in a given area of your garden? Plant a green manure/cover crop to protect the ground while you think. A green manure is a plant which you grow because it does good things for your soil, usually because it fixes nitrogen and is therefore a natural fertilizer. Again, the people who have tried cover crops in a professional setting, such as Gabe Brown[7], suggest that you should actually combine the seeds of at least seven different cover crops and sow a mixture, because of the 'diverse plants = better biodiversity" factor.

When in doubt, add more and different plants.

- Mulch your soil.

But perhaps you've planted some seedlings which you know will *become* big plants and cover a large area, but which aren't yet large, and you want to keep space open for them to grow into? You still need to

---

7.   https://www.chelseagreen.com/product/dirt-to-soil/

cover your soil surface while the plant grows to fill it. But you can cover it with a mulch of some sort. (A 'mulch' is a layer of something that isn't soil, with which you cover the soil's surface.)

By all means cover your soil with straw, hay, wood-chips, grass-cuttings or compost. This can also be the final stage of life for your 100% natural fiber clothing. Once your clothes are beyond repair, beyond even being used as dish-cloths, and ready to be thrown away, they can be used as a mulch on your soil! The worms and the soil bacteria will thank you for your waste wool, linen and cotton.

- Feed your soil.

The wisdom of the ages is not wrong in thinking that plants do require fertilizer to grow well. The mistake was in using fertilizer made from fossil fuels when we had fertilizer made from plant and animal sources available all along.

You can make compost very simply by just piling your kitchen scraps, lawn cuttings and garden waste into a pile and letting it rot down into a rich brown loam that you can pile on the soil to feed it.

You can also make fertilizer teas. Pick a whole bunch of nettles or comfrey leaves and steep them in water for six weeks. The result will be a heinously smelly liquid full of nutrients for your subterranean buddies.

If your soil is so bad—so thin and dusty that you think any subterranean bacteria are already dead, you can give it a kick start by taking a couple of tablespoons of good soil from somewhere else—ideally a woodland environment or a healthy organic garden. Put the soil in a bucket and fill the bucket with rain water. Add a couple of spoonfuls of honey or brown sugar, and let that sit with no lid on it until it starts to ferment. You'll see it start to bubble like beer. That's a sign that the good bacteria that were in the good soil are reproducing in their millions. Now you can just water your garden with the mixture, and all those good bacteria will be in your soil too.

But don't leave them to starve there! Make sure you're also adding animal by-products.

Plants and soil organisms evolved alongside animals, and they learned to eat animal by-products just as animals learned to eat plants.

Your soil will thank you for regular applications of animal manure. It will thank you if you pee on it. If you have chickens in your garden not only will your plants love the manure, but the chickens will happily gobble up all your insect pests.

There is a saying in permaculture that, "You do not have a slug problem. You have a duck deficiency." Because basically if you had ducks not only would you have eggs and manure, you would also have a flock of hungry poultry going through your garden and eating your slugs and snails.

If you don't have enough garden for livestock, however, you can get poultry manure in inoffensive pellet form. Scatter this on your soil once a month in the growing season, and watch as your plants grow healthy and your soil becomes deep and rich.

Since—in order to draw down carbon-dioxide to help solve global warming—you are cramming your garden with plants and boosting its fertility as far as possible, you might as well use that new soil fertility to grow your own food. If you grow your vegetables in the garden, not only are they as fresh as it's possible to be, but you've eliminated the impact of transporting that food to your door.

If you'd like to learn about eco-friendly ways of growing your own food in your garden. I thoroughly recommend looking further into Permaculture[8].

But perhaps you just want to have a lovely lawn and grow flowers? That's fine too. Feed your lawn and allow it to become biodiverse with different sorts of grasses, weeds and wild-flowers. Allow your borders to boil over with lots of different kinds of plants—especially native ones.

---

8.   https://permaculture.vipmembervault.com/

Feed and care for your soil, and your garden will still become a carbon sink and a haven for native wildlife.

For more information, look up the Permaculture Association[9], or just google 'Permaculture,' and you'll find enough to keep you occupied for months.

Support restorative agriculture

We can help other people to restore their soil too. Currently, farmers are growing crops in the old, world-damaging way simply because (a) they don't know any better, and (b) people buy their products and they can make a living farming in the way they do.

Just as the consumer giving up plastic means that there's now companies falling over themselves to change their packaging to recyclable or non-plastic options, if the consumer throws their buying weight behind organic and restorative agriculture, these too will thrive.

Your task, if you accept it, is to buy as much of your food locally and organically produced as you can find and afford.

Here in the UK, with our wet weather and fast-growing grass, we are in prime territory for pasture-fed, mob-grazed meat such as is produced by the Knepp estate. Check the internet to see what small farms in your area are producing organic food and support them. Many have little farm shops that it's a pleasure to visit, and many will be amenable to suggestions from regulars about the kinds of things you'd like to see.

Make local connections, so that you can get to know what's being grown near you, and support those farmers if you can.

If there aren't any local restoration farms, the next best thing is to buy organic and restoration produce from the supermarket. It probably has to travel further, but if we can get soil-supporting produce onto the supermarket shelves and keep it there, we send out a loud message to other farmers that there's a market here, and that may persuade them to change their practices too.

---

9.   https://www.permaculture.org.uk/

I've had a lot of pleasure since I started this process, because finding small shops selling local goods has anchored me in my community in a way I hadn't experienced before. I'm supporting local people in a way that I wasn't previously—artisan craft workers, small business people, the charity that grows vegetables on its own land etc. I know better what my region grows, and I am suddenly more at home in the food system than I was before when I was another anonymous shopper in a supermarket checkout line. That in itself has been a big gain if only for my own mental health.

Speaking of being anchored in the local community leads me onto my final section in this book. After all, there are a lot of things you can do as an individual to help. But somethings are done better in a group. I'm going to move on now to a brief round-up of where you can go if you've already done as much as you want to on the individual lifestyle front.

CHAPTER FIVE
Broadening our reach

YOU ARE NOT THE ONLY person out there desperately worried about climate change. As Greta Thunberg has shown, young people especially are passionate about saving our planet so we can all have a future.

In this chapter I'm going to suggest some of the things you can do to connect with others so that your individual impact can be magnified by that of others.

What are some of the things we can do together?

Find your local groups

We're fortunate enough to live in a very connected world where it's easier than ever to find people with common interests. And the nice thing about finding people with common interests is that a group of people can achieve more than a single person alone. If you want your local supermarket to stop packaging its vegetables in plastic, a letter from a thousand local residents will do more to sway them than a letter from you on your own.

Plus, if you're doing things on a community level rather than an individual one surpluses and famines tend to even out, and you get a sustained level of action.

For example, if you've planted a plum tree in your garden and you now get 20lbs of plums for one month in August, that's probably more plums than you know what to do with. If you're trying to handle them alone, half will probably go rotten before you can get to them, you'll have more plum wine and plum chutney than you could possibly want and you won't have any pears at all.

If you have a community of gardeners all helping one another, though, you can share your excess of plums with them, and they can share their excess of pears/peaches/courgettes/onions/tomatoes etc with you, so that everybody ends up better off.

Look on the internet and find your local groups. Loath as I am to recommend Facebook, it does seem to be the place where most community organizing is going on at the moment, and a search on your town name will probably bring something up to start off with.

My local area has a tree-planting group which coordinates the people who want to plant trees with the people who want to donate trees, the people who like to research who owns what bit of land so that the owners can be approached to ask permission to host trees, and the people who like to market and advertise and can go out and find new donors. Not everybody can do all of those things at once, and the good news is that with a group, not everybody has to.

My local area (Ely in Cambridgeshire) also has a Facebook group called Eco Ely[1] which gives hints on how to recycle, how to do without plastic etc, and informs us on which local shops are operating bulk buy schemes or refill schemes. It started out as just a bunch of local people exchanging tips on how to be eco-friendly, but once it gained over a thousand members it realized that it could also be a pressure group, leaning on local businesses to become more sustainable.

If you don't have an Eco [Your Town] group, why not start one? Let your local library know about it. Put fliers in your local coffee shops and before long you'll find you too are a community organizer.

Community gardening

There's almost certainly a gardening group where you live. It probably contains a lot of people who are wrecking their soil without meaning to. You could infiltrate it and use the opportunity to talk about permaculture.

Alternatively, you could start a permaculture club near you. I did that last year—again, I started through Facebook and then when enough people had joined we had a face-to-face meet up in the pub. (With Coronavirus, you may have to Zoom instead!)

Soon we were exchanging seedlings and tips on where to find free wood-chips for mulch, which local farmers/stables were happy for you to come and take away manure etc. Before long I had a speaking gig to explain permaculture to the local gardening society, and we had created a seed library for the village, to which everyone could bring their spare seeds, and from which they could take whatever they wanted.

We've established that gardening can not only help reverse climate change, but can also help provide healthy food that doesn't have to be transported for miles using fossil fuels. That's a lot of benefit for the environment that can come out of your garden. But not everyone has a garden. And there are many areas of ground in your local community that don't belong to you, and yet could perhaps become a garden for

---

1.   https://www.facebook.com/groups/315159049172004/

local people, either to grow veg or to re-wild in such a way as to benefit everyone.

The next logical step, after forming the permaculture club and infiltrating the gardening society is to see if there's some way to create a community garden for your neighbourhood.

This is likely to require a certain amount of speaking to local politicians and putting pressure on local councils, and that's where it's good that you're already in a group, because it would all be too scary to do as a single person.

It still sounds pretty daunting, I'm not going to lie. But fortunately there is help and advice available from people who have gone this way already. If doing something big in your local community really appeals to you, then I encourage you to look up the Transition Towns[2] network and see if there's a project near you, or even if you can be the one who turns your own town into a Transition Town.

Politics

We unfortunately cannot get away from politics. The people we elect to rule us are the ones who will be making long term decisions that impact the ecosystem for decades. While we as individuals cannot do a lot to impact climate change, politicians are in a position to de-fund fossil fuels and heavily invest in green technologies and restoration agriculture.

That means that voting for the politicians with the best eco-credentials is one of the most important things we can do. From the increasingly severe wild-fires, droughts, floods and other extreme forms of weather we have suffered through recently, it's becoming increasingly clear that our time to shilly-shally about climate change is running out. We need leaders who will commit to action to correct it before Australia and the US are on fire and London is drowned under the Thames. Let's let them know that we're watching, and that our planet's future matters.

---

2.   https://transitionnetwork.org/do-transition/starting-transition/

Final note

In several groups that I'm a member of, I've noticed a tendency for people who are doing a lot to berate people who are only doing a little. Vegans look down on vegetarians for not doing enough. People who are zero waste look down on those who are trying to celebrate the fact that they've started using the recycling bins instead of just throwing everything away, and so on.

The last thing we need is for everyone to get all holier-than-thou over who's being the most perfect eco-warrior. Everyone is at different stages in their journey, and not everyone can do everything. But everyone can do *something*. And if everyone does something, I think you'll be amazed at what a difference we can make together.

Good luck on your eco journey, and may our children and grandchildren inherit a better world!

[1] https://www.metoffice.gov.uk/weather/climate-change/what-is-climate-change

[2]   https://www.independent.co.uk/environment/
air-pollution-uk-transport-most-polluting-sector-greenhouse-gas-emissi

[3]   https://www.biologicaldiversity.org/programs/
climate_law_institute/transportation_and_global_warming/

Don't miss out!

Visit the website below and you can sign up to receive emails whenever Alex R Oliver publishes a new book. There's no charge and no obligation.

https://books2read.com/r/B-A-FCGL-SFKLB

BOOKS 2 READ

Connecting independent readers to independent writers.

Also by Alex R Oliver

Atlantean Devices
Atlantean Devices - Sons of Devils

Cygnus Five
Cygnus 5 - The Complete Trilogy
Lioness - Cygnus 5: Book One
Destroyer - Cygnus 5: Book Two
Phoenix - Cygnus 5: Book Three

Space Gods Saga
Starship Ragnarok

Standalone
The Witch's Boy
You Can (Help) Save The World

www.ingramcontent.com/pod-product-compliance
Lightning Source LLC
Chambersburg PA
CBHW020324290526
45785CB00007B/2911